D1795324

Related To Sex

Claire Rayner
Related To Sex

**PADDINGTON
PRESS LTD**

NEW YORK & LONDON

Library of Congress Cataloging in Publication Data
Rayner, Claire
  Related to sex.
  Bibliography: p.
  Includes index.
  1. Marriage.   2. Family.   3. Sex in marriage.
4. Sex (Psychology)   5. Sexual deviation.   I. Title.
HQ734.R27   301.42'7   78-26728
ISBN 0 7092 0686 0
ISBN 0 448 22918 8 (U.S. and Canada only).

Filmset in England by SX Composing Ltd., Rayleigh, Essex.
Printed and bound in the United States

Designed by Patricia Pillay

IN THE UNITED STATES
PADDINGTON PRESS
Distributed by
GROSSET &DUNLAP

IN THE UNITED KINGDOM
PADDINGTON PRESS

IN CANADA
Distributed by
RANDOM HOUSE OF CANADA LTD.

IN SOUTHERN AFRICA
Distributed by
ERNEST STANTON (PUBLISHERS) (PTY.) LTD.

Contents

ACKNOWLEDGMENTS   6
INTRODUCTION   7

 1   In the Beginning   9
 2   Sexual Politics   26
 3   "Legal" Sex   42
 4   In-Laws   56
 5   Parenthood   71
 6   Mothers and Sons   89
 7   Fathers and Sons   105
 8   Mothers and Daughters   122
 9   Fathers and Daughters   133
10   Brothers and Sisters   145
11   The Adolescent Explosion   176
12   Problems . . .   201
13   . . . And More Problems   220
14   Full Circle   239

BIBLIOGRAPHY   251
INDEX   253

Acknowledgments

The publishers and author would like to thank the organizations listed below for their permission to reproduce extracts from the following songs:

"I Want a Girl." © 1911 by Harry Von Tilzer Music Pub. Co. Sub-published by Francis Day & Hunter Ltd. Reproduced by permission of EMI Music Publishing Ltd., 138-140 Charing Cross Road, London WC2H 0LD.

"She Was One of the Early Birds." © 1895 by Francis Day & Hunter Ltd. Reproduced by permission of EMI Music Publishing Ltd., 138-140 Charing Cross Road, London WC2H 0LD.

"Makin' Whoopee." © 1928 by Keith Prowse Music Pub. Co. Ltd. Reproduced by permission of EMI Music Publishing Ltd., 138-140 Charing Cross Road, London WC2H 0LD.

"Tea for Two." Words by Irving Caesar/Music by Vincent Youmans. © 1924 Harms Inc. (Warner Brothers Inc.). Copyright Renewed. All Rights Reserved. Used in the U.S. and Canada by Permission. Reproduced in the U.K., and the rest of the Commonwealth, by kind permission of Chappell & Co. Ltd.

"Blues in the Night." Music by Harold Arlen/Words by Johnny Mercer. © 1941 Harms Inc. (Warner Brothers Inc.) Copyright Renewed. All Rights Reserved. Used in the U.S. and Canada by Permission. Reproduced in the U.K. and the rest of the Commonwealth by kind permission of Chappell & Co. Ltd.

"My Heart Belongs to Daddy." Words and Music Cole Porter. © 1938 by Chappell & Co., Inc. Copyright Renewed. International Copyright Secured. ALL RIGHTS RESERVED. Reproduced by kind permission of Chappell & Co.

"Always True to You in My Fashion." Words and Music by Cole Porter. © 1948 by Cole Porter. Copyright renewed. Assigned to John S. Wharton, Trustee of the Chappell & Co., Inc. Owner of Publication and Allied Rights throughout the World. International Copyright Secured. ALL RIGHTS RESERVED. Used in the U.S. by permission. Reproduced in the rest of the world by kind permission of Chappel & Co. Ltd.

Introduction

THIS BOOK MAKES NO CLAIM to be based on the results of scientifically structured studies of family behavior. There have been far too few such investigations; studies of the effects on a family of the normal attractions and tensions exerted between related members of the opposite sex – or the same sex come to that – are rarely mounted. Such information is usually discovered only as a by-product of studies into other subjects.

But as the writer of an "agony column" of a British newspaper with a readership of 14 million and the medical columnist for a women's magazine with 6.5 million readers, I deal day in and day out with "please-help-me" letters from members of families in which such tensions and attractions are creating difficulties.

It is on this experience that I base this book, and also on the face-to-face discussions I have been able to have with people with problems. Some of these were collected during the preparation of a radio series, "Families in Crisis," for the British Broadcasting Corporation (BBC); some while working on a radio documentary, currently in preparation, dealing with the problems of transvestites and transsexuals; and some discussions date from my nursing days when I was in charge of a large and busy pediatric unit and became intimately involved (in a professional sense!) with "problem" families.

Every one of the case histories, letters and accounts of family experiences in the following pages is drawn either from my own experience, or from that of clinicians I trust and know to be reliable. Of course, in each of them details, including place names, have been changed in order to obscure identities; it would be appalling if any reader were ever able to recognize any of the individuals or families. But apart from such necessary changes each case is authentic. None of them is meant, of course, to offer definitive answers to other families' problems; they are typical only of themselves. But I hope that they do, in their own way, point to possible solutions for other people. That is why they are here. That is why this book was written.

1
In the Beginning

I AM THREE YEARS OLD. I am walking along gray, wet pavements, my arm stretched high above my head so that I can hold my father's hand. When I look up at him I have to squint my eyes, he is so tall, so far away.

On the other side of him walks my mother. I can smell her scent, thick and warm, even on this cold, damp day. She is pushing the big baby carriage, and there is water in a little puddle on the cover. My sister, silly baby sister, peers over the top listening to my mother making noises at her – "Coochie, coochie" noises.

My father begins to play games with me as we cross the streets. "Upsadaisy" pulling on my arm, "downabuttercup" pushing me along. I like the game, and jump, holding on to his hand very tightly.

He swings me higher with each "upsadaisy," pushes me down harder with each "downabuttercup" and the excitement rises in me. I feel it like water, lifting higher and higher inside me, and the feeling is frightening and exciting and breathless and there is a tingle somewhere right inside my belly. I like the feeling, although I am frightened by it as well and I shriek, half laughing, half crying.

He laughs, bends down, picks me up and hugs me, and now the feelings are all good ones and I put my arms around his neck and hold on tight. "I love you, Daddy," I say, feeling myself bursting with it. "I love you. I'm going to marry you when I grow up."

My mother looks at me, peering around his big shape the way my silly sister peers over the cover of the big baby carriage.

"No, you're not," she says. "You'll go and find your own man, the way I had to." And she looks at my father and laughs, and he laughs, too, looking at her. And then they both turn their heads and look at me, and laugh that private laugh again. It is their laugh, not mine, and I am filled with feelings I cannot hold – thick, bad, angry feelings – and I kick my father against his ribs, still holding on to his neck, and he smacks my leg and puts me down on the ground again.

That is the whole of that memory. It starts in blankness and ends in a void. But it is my first awareness of the sexual tensions that can exist in a family.

It is less than 100 years since Sigmund Freud's ideas about human sexuality and its development from earliest infancy started the chain of change in the way people look at their sexual feelings and behavior. Our mid-Victorian forebears would not be able to talk to us about relationships, about the institution of marriage or about the way children should be reared, because our attitudes on these subjects would be to them totally incomprehensible. Our view of sexuality as a "good thing," something to be welcomed even in its rawest state, to be used and enjoyed as fully as possible, would make no sense to people reared from their earliest days to regard it as an expression of a despicable animality in the human that had to be suppressed at all costs. Either that, or converted by mental and spiritual effort into something "more human."

To suggest to them, as this book suggests, that within the family unit of father, mother, children and the wider kin of aunts, uncles, cousins and grandparents there could exist tensions and attractions based on that animalistic sexuality they so despised and feared would have been impossible. They would have been shocked into numb disbelief or laughed with incredulity.

This does not mean to say that none of our forebears was ever aware of the fact that sex plays a part in family relationships. Certainly Shakespeare knew – or seemed to know. His portrait of a young man torn apart by many warring factions within himself, not least of them his incestuous feeling for his mother and his sexual jealousy of his stepfather, gives *Hamlet* much of its enduring fascination.

And of course long before his time the mythmakers of Greece and Rome, and the sources from which they drew, made much of sex-based family alliances and rivalries so much so that Freud used them for the labeling of some of the sexual mechanisms that operate in all ages. There are few today who don't know what an Oedipus complex is, even if they've never heard the original Greek story.

To understand the role of sex in the family, it is obviously necessary to understand why the family exists at all. What is it for? Is it a grouping of humans that is so vital to our life and survival that it is impossible for us *not* to live in family units, or a political device forced on the majority by a few of our number for their own purposes?

Probably a bit of both. When human beings made their first stirrings toward civilization, coming down from the trees to stand on their hind legs and use their front ones to manipulate tools, they brought their primate friendliness with them. And we still have it. We need the support of a group as much in this last quarter of the twentieth century as our progenitors needed it during the Pliocene era. Solitude is and always has been regarded as an abnormal lifestyle: the hermits and anchorites who have existed throughout human history have been categorized by their fellows as mad or divine or both – certainly not fully human.

The way humanity has structured its groups over the centuries has varied, but that structure has always been an elaboration of the basic biological family – the mother and her newborn infant. Sometimes a group was made up of a number of women with babies living closely together with males living equally closely to each other, often in a special men's house, and having contact with the females only in specially prescribed ways and at specially prescribed times.

Associated with this structure has been an elaborate and often unpleasant ritual through which the adolescent boy had to pass in order to be detached from his first family of mothers-and-children and made fit to be absorbed into his second family, the male brotherhood. In this system, many writers have suggested, lie the roots of the anti-woman feeling that still plagues us. It is certainly true that many of us still put our offspring through initiation rituals at puberty – for example, the bar mitzvah and confirmation ceremonies of the Judeo-Christian religions. Today we may include young females in these ceremonies, but they were once for boys only. There is also the use of the one-sex residential school, a system of education which may be dying out, but which still exists for a select minority.

Another type of grouping was what has been called the extended family, and over which many present day sociologists sigh sentimentally, regarding it as the ideal way to live. In this, a tribe of people linked by birth and marriage were presided over by an elder, who was the arbiter of the whole tribe's lifestyle. Under his sway came his sons, and their wives, their children and their children's children. His daughters went away when they married to join someone else's tribe, though sometimes, if an elder was particularly powerful, they brought their husbands into their father's tribe. There might also have been the elder's own brothers and sisters and those of his wife if they had failed to set up their own tribes or had been cast out in some way.

Such a group could obviously consist of a great many people. Abraham's in the Old Testament comes to mind as a particularly numerous one – understandably, since he was both polygamous and prolific. And there was, before him, Noah. The remnants of this lifestyle have lingered on well into the twentieth century, particularly in some Mediterranean cultures. A familiar figure is the papa of the southern Italian countryside, who sits wrinkled in the sunshine while his family of half a dozen or so sons and sons-in-law, daughters and daughters-in-law to match, with dozens of grandchildren and possibly great-grandchildren, work the family property and defer to his wisdom.

It is not only a rural image; many tears have been shed by sociologists over the city-based extended family of the late nineteenth and early twentieth centuries. Within these the dominant figure was often a mother, very matriarchal and controlling. She did not collect her tribe under one roof but lived in her own small home with the adult children and grandchildren and their young living as nearby as they possibly could and coming to her frequently, using her as a base in all crises. Often new babies were born in her house, funeral corteges started from her front door, and wedding parties, of course, were always held "at Mom's."

This structure is admired by sociologists because it is supposed to give the young parents of the tribe, support and guidance during their vulnerable child-rearing years, and greater stability to the developing young, as well as care of the weak and elderly. When the matriarch was benevolent, this may well have been the case. When she was not, however, but was more concerned with exercising her power to her own satisfaction than with giving her adult offspring freedom to live their own lives, she was probably a malevolent influence. The sight of a man in his forties or even fifties still deferring to his mother and needing her approval and support, strikes many modern adults as depressing in the extreme.

But, for good or ill, such family groups do still exist, if in a rather more loosely knit form than they were in the back streets of New York or London in the 1930s. They have lingered particularly among certain ethnic groups, for example, Irish Catholics and Jews, and that they are still hankered after, and not only by sociologists, is undoubted. On a record album called *You Don't Have To Be Jewish*, written and produced by Bob Booker and George Foster, one sketch involves a young woman phoning her mother. She's in trouble – she's snowed in, her children are ill, the kitchen equipment is out of order, she's expecting a horde of members of her women's club to descend for lunch. The older woman soothes her, promises she will resolve all difficulties: she will struggle through the snow, buy the food, cook it for the lunching ladies and make the grandchildren well. At which point the couple discover that they are victims of a wrong number and are not related to each other at all. And the "daughter" says plaintively, "So you're not coming?"

The daughter in this case was suffering from being a member of a "nuclear family," the label used for a group made up of one adult male, one adult female and their offspring. The label is not strictly accurate; the true nuclear family is surely the mother and her dependent infant, to which the father and older, less dependent children are merely peripheral. However, accurate or not, this is the family group in which the vast majority of Western people live. And in most Western political systems this is regarded as the ideal pattern for the maintenance of law and order and the control of children, as well as for the prosperity of a highly developed industrial society. The more individual homes there are, the more consumer goods are needed: in the southern Italian extended family one large refrigerator will be enough; the same number of people split into nuclear families would need a dozen or more.

The nuclear family lifestyle is also the one to which the post-pubertal adolescent, seeking his or her own niche in the adult world, usually aspires.

Why? What causes a young man or woman to pull away from the family group in which they developed and seek to start a splinter one of their own? If, as sociologists have suggested, the extended family is the ideal and the nuclear family a stunted, stressful version of it, why should young people so willingly form their own nuclear families? Human young are neither stupid nor unobservant; if the nuclear family lifestyle were as stultifying as it has been painted, surely its offspring would hardly perpetuate it as eagerly as they do.

There can be many pressures, and sexual ones come high on the list. Traditionally, it has been the desire of young people to escape the parental nest in order to escape parental control of their sexuality that has led to the creation of new nuclear families. When the desire to escape is shared by both the young man and woman then the new family may start off smoothly enough. But sometimes there are other pressures which come into play – and sometimes it is not as easy for one of the partners to escape parental control as might be thought.

Peter and Barbara grew up in the same middle-class

suburb, belonged to the same tennis club and local young people's charity committees and were regarded by all their friends – and their elders – as a natural couple. In due course they married, while Peter was still completing his course at a technical college and Barbara, aged almost nineteen, had just finished school. She was qualified to enter a university – although she had never intended to take any further education or training. She was very much an "old-fashioned girl," she told her school counselors, who, regretting the waste of a brain, tried to persuade her to delay marriage and continue her education. But Barbara was determined to marry early, as was Peter, despite the fact that this meant they would have to live in a small, one-room apartment rather than the sort of small modern house most of the newlyweds in their suburb were able to buy. Peter knew it was only a matter of time, however; once he had his diploma a job was waiting for him at a local electronics firm, and he'd then be able to buy and furnish the couple's "proper" home.

But within a year of their wedding Peter and Barbara were seeking outside help for their crumbling relationship. Despite their four years of courtship, begun when they were aged seventeen and fifteen respectively, and the undoubted amity between them – they had a great many interests in common as well as their shared background – Peter confided in his friends when he'd had a few drinks that he wouldn't be surprised if they were divorced before he'd "worn out his wedding shoes."

Persuaded to seek expert help by one of Peter's more perspicacious friends, they eventually went to a marriage guidance counselor.

The problem, it transpired, was Barbara's vaginismus – a spasmodic tightening of the vaginal muscles when any approach was made to this part of her body. Any attempt by Peter to initiate intercourse resulted in tears approaching hysteria. There had been three times during their honeymoon when Barbara had allowed Peter to put his penis at the entrance to her vagina, but this had resulted, she said, in such excruciating pain that now if he so much as touched her she found she could not prevent her legs from clamping together and her whole body becoming rigid. She could not even allow a doctor to examine her. She had seen her family doctor in the first months of the marriage, but when she refused a vaginal examination he told her he could do nothing further. She had not gone back to the doctor since.

Peter had started to drink, and on one occasion when he had had more than usual he had tried to force her to accept intercourse. The result had been quite severe bruising of her thighs. Peter had then slammed out of the house and driven off to the local bar, where he had become so drunk that on the way home he'd crashed his motor cycle. His injuries were minor, but they'd both been very distressed and frightened by the incident. It was this dramatic episode which had finally brought them to marriage guidance counseling.

Over the next year of regular sessions with their counselor the full story gradually emerged. Peter had, quite early in their relationship, tried to persuade Barbara to have sex with him, but she had flatly refused. "What other people do doesn't matter," she told him. "I'm going to have the right to walk down the aisle in white. I couldn't look my parents in the face if I didn't."

She was an only daughter and had always been much loved – even indulged – by her parents. The family had a long tradition of church involvement (they were Methodists), though they were not unduly rigid. But they had definite views about what was right and what was wrong, views which Barbara had never questioned. To steal was wrong, to murder was wrong, to lie was wrong, and to have sex before marriage was wrong. That was the way she had been brought up, she told Peter, and her parents' example of a happy marriage showed her that such attitudes worked. They had lived their lives in that way, and they had a really lovely relationship.

It was only when the counselor probed further that Barbara began to wonder if her parents' marriage was so perfect. She knew her mother had been quite ill at the time of her own birth, and that she had been advised not to get pregnant again too soon – but in fact she had never again become pregnant. And Barbara knew her mother violently disapproved of contraception, because she had said so. She also knew that though her father was very demonstrative with her, Barbara, cuddling and kissing her easily and happily, he was never ever demonstrative with her mother, though always courteous in his behavior and speech.

Had her parents ever put an embargo on her going into their room at any time? the counselor asked.

"No," Barbara said. "Not ever," and in fact as a child she had been in the habit of wandering into their room without knocking, often in the early morning as well as in the middle of the night. "I was always a bad sleeper – I used to go to them when I got miserable, and they always let me."

They slept in twin beds and had a couch in their room which was Barbara's, when she wanted to be with them. "Isn't it possible," the counselor asked gently, "that your parents had no sex life at all? That this perfect marriage to which you aspired was based on a totally nonphysical union?"

It took Barbara many weeks to come to terms with this idea. She was eventually convinced when she managed to tell her mother of her marriage problem, having hidden it totally from her parents until then, and found her mother's response to be one of *total approval*. That was how a decent wife should be, she implied – and a decent husband didn't force himself on her. "Your father," she had said, "is a marvelous man. Some men are pigs – but your father is wonderful."

Peter was gaining insights into himself at the same time. He was the younger son, and his older brother had always been very successful. This big brother was academically gifted, had sailed through school, graduated from university with an honors degree and then studied law. Now at the age of twenty-five he was working for a very illustrious law firm, and his father was immensely proud of him. No one had ever asked his mother how she felt on the subject. She was not a woman who ever expressed an opinion, being little more than a housekeeper for the three males of the family.

Peter's own abilities were more manual – his interest in electronics had shown early, as had his lack of interest in the academic subjects his father valued. After an attempt to push Peter into the academic mold, his father had more or less lost interest in his career. But Peter was in fact doing well; he was regarded by his teachers as having a real gift for his chosen field, and they expected him to be successful in it.

His need to "prove" himself was intense. His main reason for wanting to marry Barbara was her resistance to his sexual approaches. His feeling for her now was, he was sure, genuine love, but at first it was undoubtedly the urge to "get the girl" which had pushed him into marrying her. He also gained great satisfaction from taking an academic girl out of the grasp of her teachers. Preventing her from following an academic career made his father's pride in his brother seem less important – hence his refusal to wait to marry until he was really earning enough, and his willingness to set up home on his very slender student grant. He *had* to keep Barbara away from university.

When he made his attack on Barbara he had been far from being really drunk, he now admitted, and equally far from being out of control. He had known he was being violent, but had thought a display of strength was all she needed to make her "give in." Sex and strength were much the same in his mind; certainly his father had always dominated his mild mother and to Peter this was the way it ought to be.

In addition to prolonged counseling Peter and Barbara started Masters and Johnson sex therapy, through which Peter was taught how to make love gently rather than masterfully, and Barbara was taught how to allow her own sexual feelings to be expressed rather than tightly controlled. After two years the marriage was consummated to Peter's satisfaction and without any pain for Barbara. Therapy continues in an attempt to help Barbara reach orgasm. So far she has not been able to do this, but both of them are certain that she will in time.

The strands in this fairly commonplace story are many, as is usual however typical a case history may seem on the surface. A girl reared by her sex-hating mother to be an "ice maiden" yet encouraged by her sex-hungry father to be responsive and seductive may very well marry young, throwing away other potentially exciting opportunities in order to do so. In such a girl the opposing sexual forces can be very destructive, and indeed they nearly were; Barbara drove her husband to drink enough to be at great risk of killing himself on the road – a key incident in their saga.

A young man made to feel personally inadequate by a sexually dominant father is very likely to equate sexual potency with general power and to see any attempt to prevent him from exercising that potency as a very big threat indeed. The result will be a sexual urgency that effectively prevents any exercise of tenderness or seducing behavior. In this case Peter's actions were precisely the opposite of what Barbara had been taught by her father was normal for males.

Other strands in the story include religious insistence on a *rite de passage* – a public wedding which gives the young people permission to have sex – and a fantasy image of what marriage ought to be like. This view was probably formed as much by current entertainment and culture – for example, television advertising – as by the young people's parental models. The role of parental models in the construction of a new family is, however, extremely important.

Ted, a warehouse foreman in a working-class area of East London, married Sandra, a supermarket cashier, after a short courtship. They were married within three months of their first meeting at a disco. They moved into Ted's apartment, which he had rented for many years, and seemed very content together. They had a vigorous and mutually satisfying sex life; never at any time did either of them have any problems at all in this area. Yet after ten months of marriage, Sandra had moved out and returned to her parents' home.

She sought a divorce, but her lawyer (an unusual practitioner who takes seriously the clause in the recent British Divorce Act which places a statutory duty upon lawyers to attempt to reconcile an unhappy couple) insisted she first try marriage guidance counseling. Ted was persuaded to join her and for some months they attended joint sessions, although Sandra remained at her parents' home throughout.

Ted's background was confused. His father had been

killed in a mining accident when Ted was two, and his
mother, after apparently trying for a while to maintain
herself and her child, had committed suicide. Ted was
then placed in an orphanage – a rather old fashioned
one which did not at the time of his placement operate
the houseparent system. A hundred children aged
between two and sixteen lived a communal life. (The
system was changed to small units of eight or so under a
couple of houseparents just after Ted left the orphanage
at the age of sixteen.) At sixteen, under the supervision
of a social worker, he became a lodger with a landlady
he much admired. "She left me alone, and I left her
alone," he said. "We got on fine."

At first he did unskilled jobs, having no training for
anything else, but being reliable and having a head for
figures he gradually became more and more settled
with one firm, working in their warehouse, and was
eventually promoted to foreman. He had been in this
job now for ten years and was fully content with it,
having no ambition to change. "I'm secure. I trust the
firm and they trust me. I don't need anything else. Why
drive myself bonkers trying to have more responsibilities just to earn more to pay taxes on? That'd be daft."

As soon as he was no longer supervised by social
workers, at the age of twenty-one, he had left his
boarding house and rented his own apartment, where
he lived contentedly enough, having a series of casual
sexual affairs before he met Sandra. He hadn't thought
much about marriage, he said. "I take things as they
come. I'm not a great planner." The counselor had a
distinct impression that it had been Sandra who had
taken the initiative and assumed that he would marry
her. So he had.

Sandra's background was much more settled. She was
the middle daughter in a family of eleven in which her
mother was a classic matriarch of the old school.

Every one of her married offspring lived near her, and Mum's home was still the focus of all their lives. Sandra's father, a machinist at the same firm as Ted (the couple had met through him) was a quiet, easy-going man who clearly approved of and loved his ebullient, capable and strong-minded wife. In many ways the family was very typical of the old days in that part of East London.

Sandra and Ted had, like all the other married offspring, visited Mum every weekend, when Ted would go out for a drink with his father-in-law and brothers-in-law. After two or three months of marriage, however, he began to stay away at weekends, though of course Sandra went. This caused a good deal of comment from Sandra's mother. The gaps between his visits became longer and longer, and at length Sandra had to tell her family that Ted just didn't like going to Mum's every Saturday and Sunday, though he had said that Sandra could do as she pleased.

The couple had many arguments on the subject – or rather, Sandra would harangue and nag Ted about why he didn't want to go, and Ted would shrug and say "Don't want to, that's all," and no more.

The crisis came at Christmas. Sandra had taken it for granted that he would join in these family celebrations at least, but he had refused. So she moved out and returned to live with her parents.

Counseling showed that Ted found it impossible to spend time at Sandra's Mum's without feeling "All choked like. Couldn't breathe there. Too many people, all poking into your affairs." More probing revealed that he found the atmosphere too reminiscent of his days in the orphanage when "you couldn't ever be on your own" and yet at the same time very attractive and warm. He did not respond to the warmth, however, because "they was sorry for me. Just like when I was a kid and people'd say, 'poor thing, being an orphan.' I'm not a poor thing and no one's going to say I am."

Sandra in her turn revealed a delight in being part of so large a clan, but at the same time a tangle of jealousies and resentments involving her sisters and sisters-in-law. Her need to be their equal – to have a husband and, as soon as possible, children to bring to the weekend meetings – was intense, as was her need to display her sexuality by discussing her marital sex life with the other young wives and her mother, as did the whole family. Hence the rush into marriage with Ted, who, she added revealingly, "I knew was all right because he worked with my Dad."

The counselor made several attempts to help Sandra understand the reasons for Ted's difficulty in relating to the web of extended family she found so normal, but she could not. To her, the fact that Ted had never had such a family himself should have made him grateful for the chance to be part of one. She also failed to understand that one of Ted's attractions in her eyes was the very fact that he did not belong to a family himself; she would never have to split her loyalties by getting involved with his parents and brothers and sisters, and that was comforting.

Ted was willing to try the marriage again, as long as it did not mean being sucked into Sandra's family life, but she could not accept such a condition. They were eventually divorced after the statutory time had elapsed, and three months after the final decree Sandra married her second cousin. Ted still lives alone in his apartment.

In summary then, the family structure in which most Western people now live is nuclear, made up of a couple and ultimately their children, but it is closely linked with the two other nuclear families in which the young spouses grew up and through these with a network of other relatives. In some cases this network is close and tight enough to form the extended family derived from the early human social structure of the tribe.

When young people start a new nuclear family of their own they are profoundly affected in their choices and in their adaptation to marriage and family-making by their own previous environment, by the cultural demands of the society in which their original families live and quite possibly by fantasy images based on popular films, television and romantic fiction. Even television advertisements, with their emphasis on cozy consumers living in total amity (whoever saw a family quarrel in a television advertisement?) add their own quota of stardust.

Whatever the pressures, images and ideas which may push a young couple into marriage, however, one thing is clear. Sexual need is always present in one form or another.

2
Sexual Politics

WHEN AN EARNEST woman journalist asked a Black
Power leader in the United States to define the position
of women in his movement and he said laconically,
"Supine," he was doing more than making a sexist
joke. He was making it very clear that for him and his
colleagues shared sexual need is as much a matter of
politics as a matter of love. And the huge laugh that
went up right across the world showed how many
people agreed with him.

For every couple for whom sexual intercourse is a
spontaneous and happy expression of shared loving
feelings, there is at least one other for whom it is
a weapon in a never-ending battle, a lever used in a
power struggle or currency to be exchanged in
a marketplace. How could it be otherwise? Politics
don't just happen in Houses of Parliament and Halls of
Congress. As soon as two people try to operate together,
you've got politics in action. But of course, couples do
not always realize this. Outsiders, however, can often
understand what is going on.

SEX AND POWER
Naomi and Lawrence were referred by their family
doctor in Cincinnati, Ohio to a fertility clinic after just
one year of marriage. He was then twenty-five and she
was twenty-two. At their first interview there was some

trouble. The doctor was a young woman assistant to the consultant in charge, and Lawrence was very put out by both her gender and her junior status. But Dr. Brown was very relaxed and soothing and pointed out that this was just the initial interview and that afterward he, Lawrence, would be examined by a male doctor, leaving Naomi to her care. So Lawrence agreed, if a little reluctantly, to talk to her.

He told the story of their problem while Naomi sat quietly listening to him. "We'd decided before we got married that we wouldn't delay having a baby," he said, and then he went on to point out that they weren't as young as some newlyweds, that he was earning good money with his own business – a menswear store in a busy suburban shopping area – and that they had their own beautifully furnished home, so there was no need to wait. "And a man needs a son."

The doctor was interested in his apparent need to make it clear to her that they were serious about their problem, not just silly kids in a hurry, unwilling to wait for Nature to take its course. But she said nothing and let Lawrence go on.

"We've never used any contraception, and after a year, of course, we're worried," he said.

"What about before you were married?" the doctor asked.

"How do you mean, before?"

"Did you use contraception then?"

Lawrence flushed with anger and actually stood up. "What sort of people do you take us for, for God's sake? What sort of question is that to ask?"

"I'm sorry," the doctor said mildly. "I find that most of the people who come to us have had a full sexual relationship during their engagement days."

"We're not most people!"

"I quite understand that. And I'm sorry. I meant . . ."

"Well, all right." He sat down again. "But I'll be glad to talk to your senior, as soon as I can."

When he went off to see the head Naomi stayed with Dr. Brown, and while she was examined she began to talk. In some ways she seemed quite different – chatty, cheerful and responsive to Dr. Brown's questions.

Gradually Dr. Brown found out a good deal about the young couple. Lawrence was an only son, and had always been in conflict with his father, who owned half a dozen menswear stores scattered around the city's northern suburbs. His mother had been very dominant and always worked in the business as much as her husband. In time Lawrence had become more and more resentful of any parental attempts to "run his life," and for years the three of them had squabbled both at the store and at home. "An awful life," Naomi said. "I hate arguments. Anything for a quiet life, that's me." Then she went on to talk of her own home background.

As the middle child of three, with a very beautiful and intelligent older sister and a younger, much-adored brother, she'd always felt herself to be the least noticed member of her family. "I was the dull one," she said and giggled, lying passively on the couch as the doctor examined her belly. "The boring one. But I still married Lawrence, didn't I? He's not boring. My dad never thought I'd do so well, because Lawrence's family is much richer than mine."

"How are things now with your families?" the doctor asked casually, as she got ready to take some blood for routine tests. "Are Lawrence and his parents still squabbling?"

Naomi shook her head. "They had an awful fight not long after we got back from our honeymoon. Lawrence said he wanted his own store and his father went mad. But Lawrence insisted, and he took his share of money out of his father's business on account of the work he'd done since he'd finished school, building it up, and his dad couldn't do anything, because Lawrence got a lawyer in and everything, and so he got his own store. He'll have another one this time next year, Lawrence says, now he's on his own, because his father was like a lump of deadwood, holding things back, and his mother meddled too much."

Interesting, Dr. Brown thought. She talks of *his* store – not *ours*. Aloud she said, "And now what?"

"How do you mean?"

"How are they getting on personally, apart from the business argument?"

"Well, it's the same thing, isn't it? A business argument is a family one. The same thing. So of course they haven't spoken ever since – almost a year. I don't suppose they ever will. Not till Lawrence has more stores than his father, anyway. That's what he says he's going to do before he's thirty. Mind you, with Lawrence, that could happen. He's very dynamic."

"So you must be closer to your own family now, then?" The doctor chatted on busily, as much to keep Naomi's mind off the needle going into her arm as to get the information. It wasn't really relevant to the infertility problem, after all. Or so she thought at that point.

Naomi shook her head. "He had an argument with them, too. My father said he thought it was wrong of Lawrence to fight with his dad like that, and Lawrence went mad because he said my dad should mind his own business, and my dad said it was his business on account of me needing to be looked after, and there was an awful fight. I see my parents sometimes, but Lawrence never does. He'd be mad if he knew I did. But I don't tell him. What he doesn't know won't hurt him."

The examinations and blood tests now completed, Dr. Brown arranged for Naomi to have further routine tests, at which point Lawrence came back. He made it clear that he expected to be treated only by Dr. Jenkins, the consultant, in the future. Dr. Jenkins had assured him he would and arranged further tests for him, too.

The couple came back some time later for the results of their tests. In fact, all were normal. Naomi's fallopian tubes and uterus were healthy, and she was ovulating normally. Lawrence had a normal sperm count. There were no illnesses or symptoms of any kind to provide a physical reason for their failure to conceive. Deeper probing into their sex life was obviously needed. Dr. Brown was somewhat nervous about this, after what had happened with Lawrence last time, so it was agreed that the two doctors would share the discussion with the couple. So Dr. Jenkins, Dr. Brown, Naomi and Lawrence met each other over a desk.

"We can find no physical reason why Naomi is not conceiving," Dr. Jenkins said carefully. "We've had a little discussion so far about your sexual experiences, but now I think we must go a little deeper. Does the idea of talking about this worry you?"

Lawrence went red and his face seemed to have a wooden expression. Certainly his appearance belied his words: "Not at all. As long as no one jumps to any conclusions – and as long as it stays very private. It's not something you want shouted from the housetops, is it? It's our most private business after all." Naomi said nothing, just smiled as she usually did and waited.

Dr. Jenkins began to put questions about frequency of intercourse, the positions they used, the degree of penetration, the experience of orgasm for both – and every question was answered by Lawrence. Even the one about Naomi and her orgasms. "Every time," he said, looking a little smug now. "Right from the wedding night. Every time."

"You agree, Naomi?" Dr. Brown asked.

"Do you think I'm a liar?" Lawrence looked angry.

"No. But sometimes a wife will try to please her husband by pretending."

"Not Naomi," Lawrence said confidently. "Right, doll? We have no secrets. I told you. We're not like these other people you get here. We're *us*."

The talk went on between Dr. Jenkins and Lawrence, and a picture emerged of a perfect marriage, sexually and in every other way. He was protective, tender, caring. She was loving, responsive, loyal. All that was lacking was a baby to start their family off, and all this fuss about talking over sex, Lawrence said, was absurd.

"With all due respect to your colleague," and he looked sideways at Dr. Brown, "I think a second opinion on Naomi's health is needed. You say I'm fine, and I was sure of that anyway, and you can see for yourself there's nothing wrong as far as sex is concerned, so something must have been missed in Naomi."

Dr. Jenkins and Dr. Brown then went off to confer, and they agreed that the answer was to get yet another doctor to examine and test Naomi. But, Dr. Jenkins said, he found Naomi's silence more revealing than Lawrence's chatter. Maybe if Dr. Brown could be around when Naomi came back, talk to her more, they'd begin to get somewhere.

Once he was assured that a male doctor would examine Naomi, and that the tests would be repeated, Lawrence relaxed. So much so that for the next visit Naomi came alone. He was too busy at the store, she said.

Now Dr. Brown could really talk to her, and more of the story emerged. Naomi had not only felt she was the "failure" of her family, but she'd always been aware of the lack of freedom in her life. Her older sister was allowed privileges she wasn't – on account of her age, her parents said – and her younger brother was petted and spoiled – on account of being a boy, Naomi said. As long as she could remember she'd always felt she had to be a good girl, a quiet obedient girl. If she weren't, she'd make her parents angry and would never be allowed to be as free as her big sister. And if she were *very* good, maybe they'd love her and spoil her as much as they did her brother.

It never worked, so when Lawrence turned up and was so strong and stood up to her dad – there had been many fights in the early days, long before the one which culminated in the split between Lawrence and his father-in-law – she had seen him as the answer to all her problems. Lawrence was strong and powerful and therefore safe to love. And maybe, if she were clever, she told Dr. Brown, she'd be able to get him to do all the things she wanted. She could never persuade her dad to do anything. He listened too much to the others.

"The others?" Dr. Brown asked.

"My brother and sister," Naomi said bitterly.

Anyway, her marriage to Lawrence was the best thing that had ever happened to her. To start with, she had married first – that had showed her big sister she wasn't the only one men liked, Naomi said, and suddenly giggled like a child, looking sideways at Dr. Brown, and secondly, it made her her own person. No longer would she always have to worry about what her dad was thinking and doing.

"I used to say I didn't want to have children," she said suddenly then. "Not if it meant making them as miserable as I used to be when I was little."

"Why do you want children now then?" Dr. Brown asked.

Naomi shrugged. "Lawrence does. And when you're married . . ." Her voice trailed away.

The new tests revealed nothing. Dr. Brown had been quite right in her first evaluation of Naomi's health.

There was no physical reason anyone could detect for the couple's failure to conceive.

Lawrence had a full-scale argument with Dr. Jenkins when he was told this. He called him and his clinic incompetent and stupid and accused him of hiding behind inferior staff. The couple left the clinic, Naomi trailing quietly after the fuming Lawrence, and, Dr. Brown thought, that was that.

A year later Dr. Brown changed jobs and went to another fertility clinic at a major teaching hospital in the city. One day she found Naomi's name on her list of new patients. She came alone and seemed quite pleased to see Dr. Brown.

"How have you been since I last saw you?" the doctor asked.

"Oh, just the same," Naomi said. "I've been to three fertility clinics now. They all say the same, but Lawrence reckons sooner or later we'll find a doctor with a bit of sense who'll find out what's wrong with me." She giggled her little girl giggle again. "He'd go mad if he knew I was seeing *you* here."

"Will you tell him?"

"No way! What he doesn't know won't hurt him."

"Doesn't it bother *you* to see me? After all, I failed last time."

Naomi shook her head. "No. Why should it? I don't mind."

"Do you ever mind anything?" Dr. Brown asked. "You always seem so willing to please people. Doesn't anything *ever* bother you?"

"Not really."

"People being angry? People being unkind? You don't mind?"

"No. They get over it. The least said, the better."

Dr. Brown, remembering some of their past talks, asked suddenly, "Naomi, do you *really* want a baby?"

"Of course we do. That's why I'm here."

"I didn't say *we*. I said *you*."

Again Naomi shrugged.

Still puzzled, Dr. Brown once more set about examining Naomi. It had to be done – every patient who came was examined – even though she expected to find no change. This time, however, she watched Naomi's face instead of concentrating on the physical examination, and as she covered her gloved hands with lubricating jelly in order to put her finger into the vagina, she saw Naomi grimace.

"What's the matter?"

"I hate that messiness," she said. "All that goo."

Dr. Brown was suddenly inspired. "But sex is quite messy, Naomi. Isn't it?"

Naomi nodded. "Isn't it horrible? I loathe that sticky feeling," and she shuddered.

"What do you do about it?"

"As soon as Lawrence is asleep I get up and wash, of course. I couldn't sleep myself if I didn't."

Dr. Brown took off the gloves without examining Naomi, told her to get dressed, and then settled down to a longer talk with her. She explained that while washing and douching soon after intercourse is an unreliable form of contraception (as many women have learned to their cost), it certainly doesn't make conception easy; and Naomi's fussy habits of "hygiene" had been blocking the way to the pregnancy Lawrence so much wanted. All through their two years of searching for a fertility clinic that would find out "what was wrong," Naomi had actually been preventing pregnancy herself.

But there was more to Naomi's washing than excessive fastidiousness. For all her compliance, her apparent softness and her willingness to go along with Lawrence, Naomi was, underneath, a considerable schemer. A chameleon of a girl, she had always provided just the response that was asked of her. With her parents she was the quiet, good little girl. With the doctor, the obliging chatterbox. With Lawrence a loving, tender, loyal wife as eager for parenthood as he was. But in fact she actually did not want a baby. She was also far from loyal, in Lawrence's terms, because she was visiting her parents regularly behind his back. As for being loving and responsive, she'd never had an orgasm once! But the least said, the better.

Dr. Brown referred Naomi to her marriage guidance colleagues, telling her that the problem was an emotional one, not a physical one. But, although she obediently made appointments, Naomi never kept them. She always "forgot."

But she did come back once, almost a year later, when she was sent notice of a routine follow-up appointment. The situation was much the same. The couple were still unable to conceive, and Naomi was still douching immediately Lawrence fell asleep. She was also, she said, using a new kind of lubricant, one that wasn't *too* horribly gooey, to help in their love-making, because sometimes she was a bit dry. Not that Lawrence knew that, she said – he'd be upset to think she needed any such aid, so she hadn't told him.

What she was actually using was a spermicidal jelly. All this, while still attending fertility clinics, keeping appointments made by Lawrence. She had been seen by two other doctors since her last visit to Dr. Brown.

At the time of writing Naomi and Lawrence are still in the same position. The business is growing (he has five stores now) but they have no children. He still doesn't know why she is "unable" to get pregnant, blaming the "stupid doctors," of which over the past four years she has seen a large number. Lawrence spends a lot of money on private clinic fees for this

care. Naomi still visits her parents behind his back because "They'd be upset if I didn't," and "He'd be upset if he knew."

The clear winner of this political battle has to be Naomi. And her weapon is the control of her husband's desire to extend his own empire by having a child of his own. He is clearly very interested in obvious manifestations of power. He cannot tolerate any form of control from outsiders, especially women, but he seems unaware of less overt manipulation. In fact, he is easily hoodwinked by Naomi. He still does not realize that Naomi has no intention now or ever of providing another "big sister" or "little brother" with whom she might have to compete for the attention she wants. What's more, by failing to do so she receives sympathy from her parents. They pay far more attention now to "poor Naomi" than to their son or other daughter.

It is all too easy, when talking about sex, to concentrate entirely on the pleasure aspect, but the reproductive aspect is at least as important. It is less common for a man to place a higher value on parenthood than on personal sexual satisfaction, but it is quite common for a woman to do so.

A great many women marry simply in order to have children, and once their desire for pregnancy, childbearing and nurturing has been sated they lose interest in their husbands and no longer make an attempt to find sexual pleasure with them.

It is also interesting to note how many women report loss of libido while using contraception, after a hysterectomy, after sterilization, or after the menopause. Even allowing for other psychological effects – damage to the self-image and physical illness – the ability to become pregnant clearly plays a very large role in such women's sexuality.

A role that can be enjoyed in two ways, both by becoming pregnant and by refusing to do so.

Society colludes in this. Nearly all modern, liberal abortion laws give a woman and the doctors involved in her care the right to decide, without discussion with the father of the fetus, whether or not a pregnancy will be carried to term. In Britain, under present law, women have an inalienable right to parenthood. Men have not.

But at least women today do, by and large, have some control over their own bodies as a result of easily obtainable contraception. Among my friends is a man who is one of a family of eight. His mother was a very lively, interesting lady who had been trained as a teacher, but when she married, back in 1930, respectable wives Did Not Work – that is, not for gain outside the home. Not that she didn't often say she wanted to, but every time she did and seemed ready to do something about it her husband would stop her by making her pregnant again.

"How?" I asked my friend. "She must have been there when he did it, damn it all."

"Oh, yes – but contraception such as it was then was almost always male controlled. Interruptus, or for the sophisticated, sheaths. The old man wasn't sophisticated, but he knew enough to miss out the interruptus part when it suited him. He still boasts about it now."

"How does your mother feel about it now, when he boasts like that?"

"She died when my youngest sister was born."

My friend says that's why he's never married himself.

SEX AND MONEY

Famous joke: After forty years as a successful businessman, poor old Joe lands in bankruptcy court. Woe, woe,

woe. But his loving wife throughout those forty years, his dear old Rosie, pats him on the shoulder as he leaves the court and tells him not to worry, she has a surprise for him. She takes him to a street in a classy district, and shows him a small apartment block.

"There, Joe," she says. "All ours, honey. No need to worry – we get good rents from it, believe me."

He marvels, he hugs her, and then cries, "But Rosie, where did you get the money to buy such a splendid building?"

"Listen, honey. You remember, all these years, every time we had a little bit of you-know-what you used to leave a fiver on my bedside table?"

"So?"

"So, I saved up every penny. And here it is – our own building. Security for our old age."

And Joe stares at the building, shakes his head and murmurs, "Oh, oh, oh, if only I'd given you all my business!"

Interesting fact: In Victorian times, men given to the use of slang didn't use the word "coming" to describe reaching an orgasm. They said they had "spent their lot."

Headline news: Famous film star buys captious wife – even more famous a film star than he is – another huge diamond.

Victorian novel plot: (*Dr. Thorne*, by Anthony Trollope) Heroine, beautiful, virtuous, charming, loyal, dripping with all the spiritual virtues, is poor and base born (the illegitimate daughter of a low-class though beautiful woman) but loved by son of local squire – well born, but short of money. She loves him too. Plot hinges on the need of young Frank to marry money. Plot resolved by heroine becoming an heiress in her own right. Then, and only then (after three years of agony all round) can the lovers fall into each other's palpitating arms.

Definition: Harlot – a member of the most ancient profession in the world.

Anyone with a taste for the necessary research could fill a whole book with examples of the close link that has always existed between sex and money. Men and women have been exchanging sexual favors for something else they wanted more ever since the earliest biblical times. Lilith, the name sometimes given to that subtle serpent in the Garden of Eden, has been referred to as the first harlot, but even before her time the myths of Greece and Rome were littered with characters who made a nice commercial thing out of the pleasures that sex can bring.

But never think that prostitution can only exist outside a legitimate marriage bond nor that money is always involved. Though it often is, of course, even within a marriage. There's another joke on that record *You Don't Have To Be Jewish*, in fact, two. The story of the Plotnik diamond, first. It is one of the biggest there is and worth a fortune but, says the unfortunate lady who wears the Plotnik diamond to the breathless female admirer whose eyes are glued to it: "A curse goes with the Plotnik diamond." "A curse?" breathes the female admirer. "How exciting! What is it?" "Mr. Plotnik," says the diamonded lady lugubriously.

And then there's the young married couple joke. He comes home and sings out, "Where are you?" She sings back, "I'm hiding!" And he sings again, "Where are you?" "I'm hiding!" "I've got those gold earrings you wanted. Where are you?" "I'm hiding. In the closet."

More common is a series of transactions throughout

a relationship: "Not tonight – I'm too tired." "Too tired to go shopping tomorrow? Maybe we could manage that new coat after all." That one is obvious. Slightly more subtle – just slightly – is the "If I don't get away for a vacation soon I'll be no good to anyone. How can you expect me to be all lovey-dovey when I'm feeling so worn out?" ploy.

It works in reverse as well. "Listen, after such a night out – and dinner at that place doesn't come cheap, believe me – how can you just turn over and go to sleep on me?" And then there's the husband who celebrates his promotion or a raise by being more demanding sexually, and the man who, when he is laid off or passed over for promotion, loses his sex drive altogether for a time.

During courtship days the money-sex link is even more blatantly obvious. The girls who won't even go out with a man until they've checked on the quality of the car he drives and the clothes he wears, and then only accept a second date after adding up how much he spent the first night out, are legion. The boys who take it for granted that sexual favors come in exchange for money spent are even more numerous. For quite a number of young, unattached people, the amount of sex-play a girl will allow at the end of the evening is very finely attuned to the boy's investment: the back row at the movies and a plate of chow mein at the local Chinese restaurant only warrant a goodnight kiss, while being collected in a car and given an expensive dinner before going dancing could mean a prolonged petting session to orgasm. If he takes her to the best hotel in town where he buys her champagne, and *filet mignon* and flowers, he would be most indignant if she balked at intercourse, and she knows she's in the wrong for accepting his offerings if she doesn't "go all the way."

An exaggeration? I think not. Do as I did: ask a lot of people aged between sixteen and twenty-five. And be honest with yourself about your own "hunting days."

And it's nothing new. In that most socially restricted of periods – the Victorian era – there were closely adhered to if unwritten rules about what a girl could accept as a present from a man. Take a bracelet and, even if she'd never been alone with him for a minute, she was branded as "fast" and not fit to know in polite circles.

And, of course, the giving back of presents is a very significant step and always has been. When Ophelia says to Hamlet, "My lord, I have remembrances here of yours that I have longed long to redeliver," she's telling him it's all over between them.

So from the start of any man-woman relationship that leads to marriage, certain patterns are laid down for the use of sex. Long before a couple reaches the stage of sharing a bed every night they have invested sex with a lot of subtle meanings. For some it will be an arena where they spar, and the winner of an argument will win the sexual day as well. For another it will be used as a means of control. The person in the driving seat will confer or withhold sex as a way of pushing the other partner in his or her chosen direction – sometimes without either of them knowing what is really going on between them. And for yet another – usually a woman – it is a meal ticket.

But what happens when sex becomes not merely licit, but an obligation? Within a marriage, it is often considered to be just that.

3
"Legal" Sex

"THE HONEYMOON WAS such delight, that we got married that same night," caroled Barbra Streisand as Fanny Brice in *Funny Girl*. And indeed more and more couples are choosing to share a full sexual life, even setting up home together, well before getting the public permission of a marriage, which was what their own parents generally regarded as essential. In this today's young are perhaps reverting to the practices of medieval Europe, when betrothal – the promise to marry eventually – was regarded as the entrance to licit sex. But whether today's young people are being atavistic or as modern as plastic bags is really beside the point – what is interesting is the effect such behavior has on the pattern of marriage.

David and Michelle – both in their late twenties – took considerable pleasure in being up-to-date. He worked for a record company searching out and developing new talent in the world of popular music. She was a personal assistant to a television producer. They had met at a pop music festival and, within a week of that meeting, she had moved into his apartment. They were a popular pair, gave a lot of parties, knew many minor celebrities and were sometimes mentioned in the gossip pages of popular newspapers. The apartment was furnished in the latest style, which was changed round frequently to give it a constantly new look and they wore freaky, "way-out" but expensive clothes.

After two years of living together they announced they were going to be married. They had a very noisy and fashionable wedding which was well attended by photographers. When asked by a journalist why they were marrying David said, "We thought it would make a nice change."

Six months later Michelle was found suffering from an overdose of barbiturates and rushed to a hospital. David was out of the country at the time, attending a music festival, but he returned at the news. Michelle really was seriously ill and in grave danger. At the hospital they had to work very hard indeed to ensure her survival.

When she recovered consciousness she was very depressed and at first refused to talk to David, the doctors or anyone. The hospital psychiatrist "blackmailed" her into talking by suggesting that if she did not he would have to send her away to another kind of hospital – implying a *One Flew Over The Cuckoo's Nest* type of establishment. He had no intention of doing any such thing (even if he could have found such a hospital to use, which he doubted), but he felt it was justified as a ploy to get Michelle to start talking about the cause of her attempted suicide.

She refused to talk unless David was there, and he balked at first. Why should he have to be involved? It wasn't he who'd swallowed a handful of barbiturates – he wasn't going to be clobbered with the blame for this. If Michelle was screwed up it was up to her to get herself unscrewed.

The psychiatrist used another kind of blackmail for him. "I don't mind whether you're there or not," he said mildly. "And I can probably get her to talk without you. However, you might not like what she says about you, without you there to be sure of its, well, accuracy."

Although their shared therapy had so inauspicious a beginning, in fact they did very well for the first few weeks. They overcame their initial hostility to both the psychiatrist and to each other by the time Michelle was well enough to return home, and agreed readily to make twice-weekly visits to the psychiatrist.

The core of the problem was, Michelle said, David's impotence. They had had a marvelous sex life ever since the very start of it (which in fact had been in a tent at the pop festival on the day they'd first met), and it had always been dramatic and exciting. They had made love often, and in very unusual places. They were even members of the "Mile High Club" – people who have had intercourse in an airplane in flight. But, since they had married, David's interest in sex had dwindled to the point of being almost nil, and she couldn't cope with the situation any longer.

David, however, said the problem was Michelle. She no longer made any effort to please him in bed, he said, let alone trying to turn him on. She seemed to expect him to make the first move every time, and was always passive. Her loss of verve was the direct cause of his loss of interest. Let's get things in the right order –

The psychiatrist started, in the classical fashion, asking David about his childhood experience, and David talked freely. His background was ordinary working class, he said. His father was an unskilled laborer, his mother little more than a slave to housework. He was the youngest of four children – the older three sisters were all married and settled and like their parents, and he was the family oddball. He loved them dearly, he said, though he didn't visit as often as he might, but they were great about it. "Salt of the earth," he said. "The best there are. Lovely people."

Michelle's version of his family was different. She

told the psychiatrist that David was glamorizing them. "They're not working class at all and would be very upset if you said they were. His father is an insurance agent. Unskilled laborer! For God's sake, he'd hit the roof at that! His mother is very ladylike – the house is all lace doilies and lavender-scented air spray in the bathroom – and his three sisters are just like her, married to office workers with three-bedroomed boxes in the suburbs. And so terribly boring that I can't stand them. Neither can he."

David had to admit to the truth of this eventually, when the psychiatrist faced him with Michelle's description, and then burst out into a tirade of anger. His parents *were* good people, they *were* the salt of the earth but he'd been made to despise them by people like Michelle who thought that "bourgeois middle class" was the worst thing you could say about anyone. But they were decent, clean and caring, and no worse than Michelle's own family.

Michelle's family turned out to be a divorced mother, now dead. Her father had disappeared when Michelle was three, and from then on her mother had had a few discreet love affairs. But, of course, Michelle had known about them, she said.

"Did you mind?" the psychiatrist asked.

"Why should I?"

"Adolescents often have strong moralistic views."

"Well, I didn't. Anyway, she's dead now, so what the hell does it matter? There's only an old uncle somewhere, and I never see him. I'm free, thank God. Not like David, so bogged down in awful relatives he can't breathe."

The hostilities between the couple began to increase again at this point. Over the next three weeks of therapy they squabbled more and more, and Michelle became increasingly bitter while David now showed signs of depression. He arrived, drunk, for one of the psychiatric appointments and Michelle burst into tears and hit him.

When they had calmed down, the psychiatrist learned that their shared sex life now was nil. The night before Michelle had woken to find David masturbating, and this had caused the new wave of wrath and frustration she was now experiencing.

He tried to get them both to talk about their feelings, but it was hopeless. David lost his temper and shouted at Michelle, she shrieked back, and they left separately. The psychiatrist wasn't feeling too good either.

They missed their next three appointments and the psychiatrist, somewhat demoralized by his failure, was surprised to find them turning up again, together, apparently in some amity. They talked and he commented on their relaxed, happy appearance. Michelle laughed, "David got his balls back."

"A great way to put it," David grinned, apparently quite unworried by her phrase.

"Why did that happen?" the psychiatrist asked.

"Because," David said with great humor, "we stopped listening to you, and started to use a bit of common sense."

"Well, I did," Michelle said. "I got fed up waiting around for *you* to do something to help him, so I went out and got a fella to help *me*. And I told David when I got back. And he nearly went mad, and finished up half raping me. It was marvelous."

"Just the one time was marvelous? Or have you gone on from there?"

"No problem," David said. "None at all. So you see? You shrinks know nothing. No help at all."

"If you've solved your problem, then that's great with me. But I'd feel happier for you if I could believe the, ah, cure was a permanent one. What will you do if you lose your drive again, David? Send her out to find someone else to have sex with, to start you off again?"

"Maybe. Maybe get someone else to join us, come to that." David grinned and then said, "The trouble with your sort is you're all too straight. Dull. What people like us need is more variety in our lives."

They left, and as they went through the outer office David dropped a ten dollar note. "Tell him not to bother me with his damned bills," he said. "I figure that's more than enough."

Once he was over his own irritation at the couple's insulting behavior, the psychiatrist followed up David and Michelle's progress via their family doctor who was a close contact of his. According to her, the couple's relationship became more and more stormy, and the marriage finally broke up a year after Michelle's attempted suicide. Thereafter both became involved in relationships with other people. Michelle married again and became pregnant very soon, but David remained firmly unmarried.

The psychiatrist closed his file with notes that suggested that their problem had been based on a rejection by David of the stability and the normality of his family life. His need to be different, to totally reject his conventional past, showed in many ways, not least his rough treatment of the father-figure psychiatrist. To insult him by throwing money at him, after having proven he was impotent himself (having failed to "cure" the couple) had clearly given David pleasure. Perhaps he really needed to jeer at his own father for impotence.

Anyway, the psychiatrist decided, it appeared that David was the sort of man who could not operate within a relationship where sex was legal and easily available. His stimulus was danger, in whatever form. He was proud of having had sex in an airplane in flight, which is difficult, cramped and does not allow much abandonment. People who find that sort of sex enjoyable, the psychiatrist concluded, are more interested in the trappings of it, especially the risk of being caught, than the reality of the feelings involved.

As for Michelle, she colluded in David's rejection of "straight" living and "straight" sex, but only up to a point. That she put a higher value on licit sex than he did was made clear by her method of "curing" him – having an extramarital sexual adventure she flaunted it at him as a way to bring him back into line. But did she, to an extent, also see married sex as boring, tedious, not worth the effort? After all, she had been reared by a woman whose own married sex had been taken away by an absconding spouse, and who had only ever had *discreet* extramarital sex thereafter. Would this have given Michelle the idea that only sex *outside* marriage would satisfy? Not really, the psychiatrist decided, because if she had such an idea why react to loss of married sex with a suicide attempt? And, why marry again so soon after losing a husband? It seemed that it was married sex she wanted more than a particular spouse.

The psychiatrist finally added the file to his collection of what he called the "Mr. and Mrs. Syndrome" – people who cannot cope with the role of married man and/or married woman, and who suffer sexual problems as a result. Although this case was a very extreme form of it, it was still a classic case for all that.

That married sex can be tedious is a well-known fact exploited by every stand-up comic there ever was, but the question is, is it the sex itself that is dull, or the people in the marriage?

Harold Pinter explored this theme in his play *The Lover*. A conventional married couple bid each other farewell at the start of the day. We then watch the wife welcome her lover and see clearly how much fun and excitement they share. At the end of the day, the husband returns to the marital home from his bread-winning activities, and we discover that in fact the husband and the lover are the same person. The couple have been fantasizing a secret love life with which to keep their married sex exciting.

Is this licit sex, or illicit sex? That some people seem to need a definition is very clear. Married couples are constantly asking advisers on newspapers, magazines and phone-in radio shows for definitions of what is "right" and what is "wrong" in married sex. Interestingly, it is comparatively rare for a single man or woman to ask for the same sort of definition. Even in an age of greater sexual freedom, the majority of single people in a sexual relationship seem to feel they are in the wrong anyway, or that the old value judgments are irrelevant, and for these reasons perhaps ask for fewer definitions of what is permissible. It's as though people see sex as qualitatively changed by the partici-pants' civil state.

Dear Claire,

I don't know how I can bring myself to write this letter. I hope you won't think badly of me because of what I'm going to ask you, but I don't know anyone else I can ask. Let me start at the beginning so that you'll see I'm a decent woman, not the sort who would usually have a problem like this. I am thirty-seven and until I was twenty I lived in a village in the north of England with my parents. It was a lovely childhood, even though times were hard, lots of love and care always, but strict as well. Don't get me wrong – my mother wasn't the hard kind or one of these child batterers, but she made it clear there was a right and a

wrong way to live and woe betide us if we didn't
remember it. I was nineteen and she still wasn't above
taking a slipper to me because I got in late. Actually,
the bus had broken down and it wasn't my fault, and
when she heard from the neighbours that what I'd
told her was the truth she was very upset and never
again got angry like that. But I respected her for it, I
really did. None of this permissive silliness was allowed
to spoil my life, or my brother's. Well, when my dad
died in 1960 we had to come south to live, because my
uncle was in London, and he was our only relative. He
died five years ago, by the way, just after my mother
did. That's really why I'm writing to you, in a way. If
she were still alive, I'd have her to talk to and she'd
soon put me right, I know. But she's gone and I'm as
good as alone.

I got married when I was twenty-five and we were
very happy always. Michael is a quiet sort of man, not
pushy and noisy, and very steady. He's worked for the
same firm since he left school, he's in engineering, and
has always been a good provider to me and the children. He's never gone out with any other girl, ever – I
was his first girlfriend, as he was my first young man.
He's a marvellous father to our two boys, who are now
ten and eight.

So, what's the problem? you may be asking. It's the
way Michael has changed. We have always had a good
intimate life, or so it seemed. There have been times
when the children were small when I was tired and not
so willing but usually I am responsive and I supposed
he was as satisfied as I was. But last month I was clear-
ing out his shed in the garden to surprise him and I
found these disgusting books – you know the sort,
women in suggestive poses and men as well. I was so
upset I just stood there and didn't know what to do. I

then thought suppose the boys find them? and at once I put them on the bonfire.

When he came home I decided I wouldn't say anything, how could I possibly say anything? But it was obvious something was wrong and when we went to bed, well I couldn't bring myself to get into bed with him, I felt so bad, and it all came out. He told me the books were not important – that all the men at work read them for a laugh, so he did too. And he told me I was old-fashioned and not to worry so much. Well, I thought, he's probably right. With an upbringing like mine, I dare say I am a bit stick-in-the-mud, and I've got to make an effort to be up-to-date and so I said it was all right and we'll say no more and he of course promised not to bring such filth into the house again. That was a month ago and I thought we were back on the same footing, though I'd had to work at it, I can tell you, and then last night he really upset me. We were in bed and he suddenly said it was time I got rid of some of my old-fashioned ideas and made life more interesting for both of us. He went on and on, and said he loved me very much and all that, but I needed to get a bit more education, and then he suggested we do things that I can't even write down in a private letter, they're so awful. He's gone to work now and said he's bringing home some of these education books as he calls them and that we'll have some fun, but honestly, how can I? I love him, I know he's a good husband and all that, but he's made me feel like a piece of dirt, not like his wife. That's the way men treat prostitutes, not decent wives, surely. I know times have changed, but not that much, certainly not for me. How can I go on in my marriage with all this happening to my husband? How can I get us back to the happy way we were before these horrible books put filthy ideas into his head?

Dear Claire,

My husband and I have always had a good and varied sex life and been very adventurous but there is something now I'm a bit worried about. He has said he wants to advertise for another couple to share with us some things – we've read about this sort of thing happening and we're adventurous as I said. But the thing is, could it make trouble in any way? We have two children, Dawn is six and Darren is five, and of course their welfare comes first. I just don't know if what we are thinking of is really legal.

Dear Claire,

My wife has always been shy about sex, and I've had to teach her a lot. She's tried to overcome her mother's attitudes (*she* thinks kissing in public is filthy!) and, bless her, she's been marvelous. But I can't persuade her to have sex anywhere except in bed, at night. I've told her over and over it's all right, we're married, it's our house, no one can ever see us if we make love on the rug in front of the fire in the living room, but she says she feels it's all wrong. I think if *you* told her it was all right, she'd listen to you. And it *is* all right, isn't it?

Dear Claire,

My husband keeps on trying to get me to have sex with him in the backwards way, and is getting more and more insistent about it. I don't fancy the idea at all, but it isn't that that worries me. I mean, I can deal with my own feelings, but something I read the other day in a magazine worried me. We have two little boys, you see, and I read that this sort of sex is what homosexuals do. Could they have been affected by this thing in him? Can it be inherited?

Dear Claire,

It's all very well for you to write in an article like that one in last week's magazine about children learning about sex in the most natural way by seeing their parents cuddling each other and kissing, but what about people who do not naturally behave like this in front of an audience? For me, it's as embarrassing to kiss my husband when others are near as it would be to actually lie down and have intercourse with him, and you wouldn't suggest parents should do that in front of their children, would you? Or are you in fact saying they should? Because you'll never convince me or any other decent mother that that is good sex education.

Dear Claire,

I thought I'd write to you again about things here with us, since you were kind enough to answer my last letter. I did as you suggested and talked to Keith about going to marriage guidance and we did, and they seemed very understanding about his need. They said that cross-dressing isn't all that unusual, that quite a lot of men have this need to express the feminine part of their natures by putting on women's clothes sometimes, and if I could be tolerant this need not damage our marriage. Well, we went on much the same but I did feel that now Keith knew I was prepared to make an effort to understand, he stopped trying to control it. I mean, he was dressing up every chance he had, and now he says he sees no reason why the children shouldn't see him, because it would help them to be more tolerant of the wide range of normal human sex if they saw him. But I don't know – it bothers me. I feel funny seeing him like that, so how could they not feel peculiar? Anyway, he's promised me we'll go back to the marriage guidance before he does anything about the children.

One thing that dealing with a newspaper problems page teaches you is that there is no such thing as unusual sexual practice. Whatever kinky idea Joe Smith comes up with, some hundreds of other Joe Smiths have thought about it before him, are thinking of it at the same time or are getting ready to think about it tomorrow. The range of normal sexual expression is infinitely wide. Perhaps because we are so adaptable, so big brained and therefore so curious, we have converted our reproductive behavior, with its built-in incentives to create new human beings, into the greatest of human sports. Whatever pleasure it gives can be enhanced by variation and we enhance it for all we're worth, all the time, everywhere.

The likelihood is that we have been operating in this way for a very long time, probably ever since we first got down from the trees and up to our hind legs. Admittedly it is only since the twentieth century provided us with really effective birth control that we were able to totally divorce the recreative aspects of sex from the purely creative (in a biological sense), but even long before then, when childbirth was an almost inevitable result of human heterosexual activity, we were right in there playing games.

Yet we still need in every generation to spell out new rules by which to play, new definitions of what is all right and what is out of bounds. We "inherit" some ideas from our parents, of course; as these pages have already detailed, there are few aspects of a person's life that are not profoundly affected by childhood experience and therefore by parental behavior. But we modify these childhood experiences by what happens to us later, and then in our turn we hand on our ideas to the children we launch. And however liberal we may think we are, however enlightened, among those attitudes will be clear statements about what is right and what is wrong when it comes to sex. Interesting, isn't it, that the word morality is almost always used in reference to sexual behavior, but hardly ever to working behavior, social behavior or even financial behavior?

4
In-Laws

FIVE HUNDRED YEARS AGO the phrase mother-in-law meant a stepmother. Now it means – what? It is an odd phrase, carrying a wealth of meaning, yet having no real legal status. For example, a father or mother-in-law has no special rights whatsoever. Should a child-in-law die intestate and have no other relations at all, neither would be able to claim the estate; they have no legal status as kin despite the label.

Similarly, with one notable cultural exception, they exist as kin only in relation to the spouses of their offspring. That is, by becoming her son's wife's mother-in-law, a woman does not automatically become related to other members of the girl's family. The notable exception is in the Jewish community. Here a relationship is recognized to exist between the two sets of parents whose children have married each other, and it has been dignified with its own label: the mother of a married daughter may refer to her son-in-law's parents as "my *mechutanim*" (the feminine singular is *mechutanista* and the masculine is *mechutani*), and vice-versa.

Legal status may be missing from the mother-in-law's role, but emotional meaning is not. For centuries "my wife's mother" has been seen as a source of strife, a meddling intruder who will do all she can to spoil a married man's love life, alienate him from his wife and children, and prevent him from drinking, smoking and doing anything enjoyable while expecting him to work unremittingly in order to pile all his earnings at his wife's feet. And "my husband's mother" too has often been regarded as a jealous, wicked old harridan who treats her son's wife with hostility, suspicion and scorn.

Interestingly, fathers-in-law have had nowhere near as bad a press. Indeed, in popular mythology they are often seen as potential allies of the downtrodden younger spouse. Jokes about fathers-in-law run along the lines of "Poor guy, he's got to live with her *all* the time."

This anti-mother-in-law feeling may be an expression of anti-woman feeling, an offshoot of the same deep suspicion of the mother figure (born of primitive goddess-worship) that gave medieval people witches to chase. The sin perhaps is to be a peri-menopausal woman, rather than to have children of marriageable age. From time immemorial, middle-aged women have been regarded either as a threat or a joke (and, of course, laughing is the ideal way to defuse a threat).

There have been a few exceptions of course. The biblical story of Naomi and Ruth comes to mind. Their's has always been seen as the story of a close and supportive love between a woman and her daughter-in-law. However, close study of the biblical passages reveal a rather different situation. Naomi was a widow who had the added misfortune of having both her married sons die. One daughter-in-law returns to her own tribe, but Ruth, the other, clings to her mother-in-law with the famous "whither thou goest I will go" speech. Then Naomi, by advising her daughter-in-law very precisely on her behavior, gets a rich husband for Ruth. Boaz was a kinsman, and there were certain statutory obligations on him to marry the helpless young widow, but all the same it was Naomi's careful scheming that ensured that he fulfilled them. Ruth then obligingly became pregnant. In ancient Jewish law, this child was regarded as being the offspring of Ruth's dead husband and therefore of his family. The Book of Ruth ends tellingly, "And the women of the neighborhood gave him [the baby] a name, saying, 'A son has been born to Naomi . . .' "

So if you study the story carefully it once again makes it clear that middle-aged mothers-in-law can be self-seeking and manipulative to a marked degree.

Dorothy was twenty-nine when her husband died of cancer, leaving her with one daughter, then aged eight. She had no other relatives living near her, since the couple had emigrated from Scotland to Ontario when they married, and their families left behind had been indignant enough at their departure to break off contact. Her own parents were dead, anyway, so in effect Dorothy was alone in Canada.

In fact, as a very pretty girl she was popular, and as her husband had been insured in order to leave her comfortably off, she was also approved of by her neighbors. Considerable efforts were made by them to look after "poor Dorothy," and for the next ten years she lived a pleasant social life, meeting eligible men, seeming often to become close to them, but then steering away. She would confide in her friends that "Gloria needs me too much for me to marry again. She's lost her father, poor darling – she's entitled to have me to herself." This attitude was to an extent admired by her friends, who knew good mothering when they saw it, but they still felt it worthwhile trying to help "poor Dorothy," and so went on and on finding new men to introduce to her.

The ten years passed happily enough for Dorothy, who incidentally improved her finances considerably with the aid of advice from her friends and from the men to whom they introduced her on how to invest her income. She never needed to go out to work while Gloria was growing up, and she never seemed to be short of cash. But there was always someone to take "poor Dorothy" and Gloria along to their summer cottage for a holiday, someone to make sure "poor Dorothy" and Gloria had a good Christmas or Easter or whatever.

When Dorothy was thirty-nine, Gloria married. Dorothy had for some time been telling her friends that Gloria was a trial to her – sullen and selfish, she would say, a rebel without a cause. "After all I've done for her," she would say sadly. "I gave up my chances to find personal happiness over and over again for Gloria's sake – yet she treats me like this. Ah well, at least her poor father didn't live to see it happen."

Gloria's husband Henry was eleven years her senior, a successful pharmacist in the process of building his own production company; he developed and marketed Health Food Supplements and Herbal Remedies which were harmless, if not entirely as efficacious as they might be, and were certainly fashionable. So there was no shortage of money. He had elderly parents living on the remote West Coast and one brother who was away in the army. He had met Gloria while she was at Toronto University studying for a biology degree. He had built much of his success on his shrewdness in spotting young talent and tying it up, and he had been looking for new graduates to work for him. He had not offered Gloria a job (as a freshman year student he wasn't interested in her in that way) but had chased after her with considerable determination from the moment he first saw her. She was as pretty as her mother.

The wedding was big and expensive and her friends

all agreed that Dorothy was incredibly brave throughout. Not yet forty, and all alone – but Henry was marvelous. He told everyone in his bridegroom's speech
that his affection for his mother-in-law-to-be was part
of his love for his new wife, for wasn't Dorothy a
mother-in-law to be proud of ? So charming, so devoted,
so *good*. Applause greeted this, and then Henry said
that from now on, Dorothy's address was the same as
his and Gloria's. Once they were back from their
honeymoon, he was determined that Dorothy would
move in to share their home. No stupid mother-in-law
jokes for this pair of newly-weds! Dorothy seemed overcome by this and protested that she did not want to be
a burden on the young people, but Henry was adamant.
And while Dorothy's friends told each other how lucky
she was to have so marvelous a young man marry her
daughter, they could see, from the expression on
Gloria's face, just what a bad time "poor Dorothy"
had had with her. Mind you, from now on, with her
married to Henry, it would be different. He'd keep his
young wife in line, and as a married woman herself
she would be different. She'd be grateful to have her
mother's help now in running the big new house
Henry was buying, and of course later the babies would
start arriving.

However, Gloria insisted on going back to the University after the honeymoon, and this created a considerable family argument. Dorothy backed Henry;
admittedly she had given up a lot to get Gloria educated
to university level, but now that she was a married
woman it just wasn't right. Gloria pointed out sharply
that her mother had had to make no sacrifices to edu-
cate her, since she had won grants and scholarships
right from the start and could still study under her own
steam whether Henry agreed or not. She wanted to be
married to him, of course she did, but she saw no reason

why she should tie herself down to domesticity so soon, and with her mother living in the house, there'd be little enough for her to do anyway. She added, "You never let me do anything."

Dorothy wept and said she "had only ever wanted to look after her only little one," but she told Henry that maybe Gloria was right after all; she needed to get this restlessness out of her system. "Let her get her degree," she advised him. "Then she'll settle down."

So for the next three years Dorothy ran the house while Gloria studied, and Henry seemed content enough. His friends said he should be, with two devoted women looking after him, and he would grin and agree that the situation had a lot going for it. Indeed, he had found that the little edge of rivalry between his wife and his mother-in-law did him no harm. He was exceptionally well looked after, and his life was very peaceful. Gloria had soon learned that in any disagreement between herself and Henry, he would get her mother to line up on his side, and Dorothy too found that if she tried to cross Henry in any way she would have both him and Gloria ranged against her. So the three of them settled into a pattern that seemed to suit them all fairly well.

Once Gloria got her degree, Henry said he wanted to start a family. He was now thirty-two to her twenty-one, and it was high time. Gloria in due course had a son. She was ill after the baby's birth and had to be readmitted to the hospital – she had an infection. Dorothy told the hospital that she would look after the baby at home, instead of having him readmitted too, to make it easier for Gloria. The hospital doctor agreed and overrode Gloria's objections. She was breast-feeding the baby and wanted to continue doing so, but she was feverish. The doctor thought the arrangements available for the baby's care were good and said that Gloria should be freed of the responsibility until she was well.

She tried to reestablish breast-feeding on her return home but failed completely, and the baby went back on the bottle. For the next few weeks the tension built up considerably between mother and daughter over the baby. Gloria was undoubtedly unwell. Her infection had been cleared, but she was still anemic, tired easily and was often depressed. Dorothy said that she would look after the baby to give Gloria a chance to recover, but Gloria said she didn't want that – she'd recover at the same rate whether she was looking after the baby herself or not. But Henry intervened and, with the back-up of the family doctor, decided that he and Gloria should go away so that she could have a long rest.

They went to stay at a quiet hotel in the mountains, and each evening Henry would phone Dorothy for a bulletin on the baby. Gloria seemed less and less interested in her son's welfare, however, and one night suddenly shrieked at Henry that he "loved that damned baby" more than he loved her.

Henry was shocked and said so. They had a big argument, and he stormed out of the hotel leaving her alone in their room. When he returned three hours later (having, as he said, stayed away to give her time to think about how badly she was behaving) he found she had taken an overdose of her sleeping pills.

She was admitted to the hospital again and diagnosed as suffering from postpartum depression. She underwent various treatments, including ECT (electric shock treatment). It was fortunate, everyone agreed, that the baby wasn't suffering. Dorothy was looking after him very competently.

Gloria returned home for a weekend visit three months after the onset of her illness, but she did not respond well to this, and it was agreed that she needed further hospitalization. It was not until the baby was almost nine months old, in fact, that she was regarded as fit enough to return home for good.

After much family discussion it was agreed that Gloria would go to work. She herself felt her problem might be that she was not a "home body" like her mother. She got a job teaching biology at a high school, where she is now head of the biology department. She enjoys her work and has no intention of ever giving it up. She and Henry have agreed that they should have no more children since their son's birth had made her so ill. Dorothy continues to run the house and look after the little boy, now five, and Dorothy's friends agree that it has all worked out well; thank God poor Henry and Gloria had her to lean on. Mind you, they say, Dorothy doesn't have as much fun as she might – for a woman of her age, to have the full responsibility of a little boy (a difficult, willful child who sleeps badly and is very fussy about his food) is not easy. She doesn't go out as much as she used to, but as Dorothy herself says, it's enough to provide a home for Henry, little Robbie and, of course, Gloria.

It is more an indictment of the way Western society is structured than of women themselves that so often middle-aged women do meddle so destructively in the lives of their adult children. Despite the women's movement we persist in overvaluing feminine youth and the functions of childbearing and childrearing, while at the same time undervaluing feminine intellectual and creative ability. The best that widowed Dorothy's friends could do for her was suggest a re-creation of her married state – they pushed her in the direction of potential new husbands rather than to interesting activities of her own, and even then they were very ambivalent. They *approved* of Dorothy's "devotion" to her daughter as displayed in her refusal to remarry. Women in Dorothy's position can't win, on a personal level. They can only operate through others, can only find their satisfactions in vicarious living. Although perhaps not too damaging when a child is young, this can be disastrous when the child reaches sexual maturity. Much of Gloria's tragedy – the loss of her child, the alienation of her husband – was due to Dorothy's behind-the-scenes manipulation. Yet who can entirely blame Dorothy? What else was there for her? Society, in the shape of her friends, manipulated her as surely as she manipulated her daughter, son-in-law and grandson. By apportioning their approval and disapproval as they did, they pushed her along her destructive path – destructive, that is, for the younger family, but reasonably creative for her. She at least gained a surrogate husband, hers in all but sex, and another child to rear.

In many ways, of course, the parent-in-law role is an impossible one to fill. If the parent behaves as a friend to the young newcomer to the family, there is a risk of the friendship ripening into a more intimate feeling, expression of which can explode the relationship between the young people involved.

Susan was eighteen when she married Danny, who was twenty-five. Susan's mother and father, Nina and Andrew, were young and lively – they were both aged only thirty-eight and dressed and behaved like much younger people. The four of them got on very well, went out together often, laughed at the same jokes and altogether had a great deal in common. They were, as a family, much admired and envied by other young people in whose families traditional parent-in-law tensions were showing. As Danny's best friend said,

"Here am I having to kow-tow to a woman I don't like, and even having to call her Mom while she pokes her damned nose into all my business, and there are you with a smashing chick you call by her first name to hang on your other arm, with your wife's approval! Some guys have all the luck."

But within two years both the young couple's marriage and that of the parents had broken up. Susan had become pregnant and, very sick throughout, had had to be admitted to the hospital for the last three months to protect the pregnancy and bring it to term. Nina had "done her best to keep the poor boy happy." One night while Andrew, who was on shift work, was at the factory, Nina and Danny had a few drinks together at her home. Danny had become fairly drunk and made a pass at Nina – and she had responded. Andrew came home, caught them kissing, and beat Danny up. When Danny visited Susan the next day she was upset by his black eye and bruises, he told her what had happened, complaining about her father's behavior. It had meant nothing with Nina, he said. He had been miserable and they'd had a few drinks, nothing to make a fuss about. And in the circles in which they moved such casual behavior was accepted as harmless – *between friends*. But Susan *did* make a fuss. There was a terrible scene with her mother, and Susan insisted that Danny move out of their apartment. By the time the baby was born Andrew had thrown Nina out of their home as well, and the four were scattered and irreconcilable.

If Nina had been like the busybody who insisted on being called Mom, it is exceedingly unlikely that Danny would have ever felt she was sexually desirable or approachable, however young and pretty she looked. It was her total abrogation of any maternal role that made her accessible to him, and he was highly indignant when his father-in-law beat him up. As far as he could see – and he was not a young man much given to deep insights – he'd behaved as anyone in his situation would when offered the comfort of a little extramarital play at a time when his wife was unavailable. And while a friend might be annoyed at someone's attentions to his wife, he need not have behaved as violently as Andrew had. Danny could not see that Nina's relationship to him was relevant, nor, apparently, could Nina. But to Susan, herself on the brink of motherhood, and to her father – who had suffered the added indignity of being cuckolded on his own territory, in his own house – it was very relevant indeed. Andrew had reacted as a father would to a recalcitrant child – the beating was delivered by a dominant male to a pushy adolescent. And Danny, feeling this, was bitterly offended.

But most of us would have seen Nina's and Danny's behavior as "wrong"; we graft on to the parent-in-law role the same sexual taboos we recognize in the parental role, and feel that people who deliberately fail to define the parental aspect of the in-law's position are asking for trouble. Indeed, to be a successful parent-in-law is far from easy; the relationship must tread a narrow line between kinship and friendship; overstep in either direction and the result is trouble.

Difficult as it is for the parents-in-law themselves, it can be even more difficult for the young people. Sometimes young couples are hurt by accident – they become emotionally involved with each other in spite of the fact that their respective parents are already at "daggers drawn." The classic example is, of course, Romeo and Juliet; those star-crossed lovers suffered as they did simply because their parents and families were feuding.

But they do not exist only on a stage or in the pages

of a script. Over and over again young couples meet and marry across the boundaries set by their parents and head bang into misery. The Jew who marries a Gentile, the Protestant who marries a Catholic, the black who marries a white, the poor who marry wealth – they may be happy together as long as both sets of parents are tolerant, even if the society in which they live is not so. But if there are parental objections, the resulting strains can tear the family fabric apart, and sometimes the marriage, too. Rare is the individual who can comfortably choose between parent and spouse and live serenely thereafter without guilt or distress.

This adds yet another dilemma to the parent-in-law role. Often they must either swallow abuse and/or rejection of their deeply held beliefs and prejudices, and let their adult children go their own way without a murmur, or see those adult children unhappy and alienated from them. Losers, all down the line.

Other in-laws who are sometimes forgotten, who can be at least equally important, are sisters- and brothers-in-law. The relationship between siblings is complicated enough, heaven knows (and in chapter 10 this subject will be considered in more detail), but that between the spouses of siblings can be even more so.

Here again there are traditional attitudes. A classic figure of fun is the wife's lazy, indigent brother. Another example from the record *You Don't Have To Be Jewish* (this is a gold mine of typical family attitudes) is a sketch called "Reading The Will" in which a family listens to a rich man's disposition of his fortune. There is a bequest to "my wife's brother, Louie, who lived with us for thirty years, who never did a day's work in his life, but knew better than anyone how to handicap the ponies, to my dear brother-in-law Louie, who said I'd never remember him in my will – hello, Louie!"

Irish folk tradition also abounds with stories about

wives' shiftless young brothers, as does the Italian. These have one thing in common with the Jewish pattern of family life; they all regard the extended family as a Good Thing and take family responsibilities seriously. They also derive from an environment of deep poverty. However rich the present generation may be, there is usually a common family memory of days when the old couple were poor, there were many children, and the oldest girl automatically became her mother's assistant. The "little mother" who dragged her younger siblings around with her is part of all these ethnic traditions. She was also much in evidence in the slums of London, as cartoons from *Punch* in the 1890s show.

One obvious example is a beautifully drawn cartoon of a scrawny girl of about twelve with a toddler in one arm, pushing a makeshift baby carriage, and with two urchins clutching her skirts. She is glaring furiously over her shoulder at yet another urchin who is struggling for his life in the frozen-over pond in the background, having just fallen through the ice. "Come on 'ome this instant," the caption reads, "or I'll tell Mum you got your feet wet!"

That little girls brought up like this should take it for granted that they had to provide homes for their lazy brothers is natural. It is interesting, however, that never at any time is it suggested that unmarried sisters-in-law who move in with a young couple are a burden in the same way. There is an equally long tradition of the useful maiden aunt, the drudge of the household, who pays for her keep with her labor. Few husbands complain about *them* in the old jokes and stories the way they do about brothers-in-law. Could this be only because females have, by and large, been reared to be useful in a domestic sphere, and therefore are not seen as burdens? Or because females pose no sort of threat, sexual or otherwise?

Indeed, a sister-in-law can be a sexual benefit around the house, as Charles Dickens found. His wife Kate, rapidly worn out by excessive childbearing, became petulant and unhappy. Georgina, her younger sister, became Dickens' "angel of the fireside" in every way – including, it is widely thought, sexually. Certainly she ran his home and cared for his children until she died at a fairly young age, plunging Dickens into a grief from which he took a long time to recover, if he ever really did.

For many years in England there was a great deal of discussion about the closeness of the relationship between sisters-in-law and brothers-in-law. In the first half of the nineteenth century it was illegal for a man to marry his deceased wife's sister; this relationship was listed in the "Tables of Affinity" at the front of the Book of Common Prayer as a case in which the individuals were forbidden to marry. These are sometimes called the laws of consanguinity.

In 1850 a proposal was put before the House of Commons to make such marriages legal, but it was defeated. It was then brought before the House of Commons again no fewer than twenty-eight times over the ensuing fifty years and was defeated each time. One cannot help but wonder who was so interested, and for so long, in the passing of such an Act. But, whoever was involved, it was not until 1907 that the Deceased Wife's Sister Marriage Act was finally passed, making such a marriage legal. Even that Act looked nervously over its shoulder at the Church – it was Church views on incest that had for so long blocked the new law – and allowed clergymen the right to refuse to officiate at such a wedding if it went against their consciences, which for many it did. The views of Edward Bouverie Pusey, the great Oxford theologian, prevailed. He had opposed the law in the 1880s and commented then that if such a law were passed the question would have to be considered "whether *any* affinity is a hindrance to marriage. If marriage with the deceased wife's sister is legalized, I do not see how any other marriage with one connected by affinity can be consistently maintained to be illegal." The fear of incest clearly loomed large in many educated minds of the nineteenth century.

And it still does. To this day, letters arrive at magazines and newspapers asking nervously whether it is "wrong" to have a relationship with a sister- or brother-in-law, which demonstrates very clearly just how confused many people feel about this ambiguous relationship. It is a kinship, and yet it is not. People linked by such a tie ought not to feel any sexual interest in each other – but often they do. As a waggish journalist once wrote when one of the famous, beautiful and very look-alike Gabor sisters was married for the umpteenth time, "Poor man! When he visits his in-laws for Sunday afternoon tea, how will he ever be able to decide which of the luscious lovelies is his to take home?"

The result of this widely felt confusion about the sister- and brother-in-law relationship is a broad vein of popular distrust similar to that felt about mothers-in-law, though not quite as deep or as strong. Like the mother-in-law jokes that express that feeling, the jokes about sisters- and brothers-in-law are based on genuine uneasiness and exist to defuse a threatening situation. How many people reading this who have brothers- or sisters-in-law can say, hand on heart, that they are totally comfortable with them? Very, very few. Suspicion and anxiety hover over this relationship for almost all of us.

5
Parenthood

THE BOOK OF COMMON PRAYER has no doubt about it. The first and most important reason for marriage is "for the procreation of children, to be brought up in the fear and nurture of the Lord." The second is "for a remedy against sin and to avoid fornication that such persons as have not the gift of continency might . . . keep themselves undefiled." Neither of these reasons is precisely joyful or loving, yet they are shared by all Judeo-Christian religions. The Catholic church holds to these beliefs with such enthusiasm that attempts to avoid procreation can lead to all sorts of religious penalties.

It is not only religious dogma that puts childbearing at the top of the list of important factors in a marriage. So do most people. The childless marriage is regarded with great suspicion or pity by outsiders. If a couple won't have children then they are selfish; if they can't, they are deprived and pathetic. Even people with a low opinion of the joys of parenthood and little taste for the company of young children feel pressured into pregnancy once they are married. The unspoken (though occasionally voiced!) question to the voluntarily childless is "Why bother to marry if you aren't having children?"

That marriage and childbearing go hand in hand in the popular mind is borne out by the way some liberal couples who live together without bothering to marry rush to the nearest registry office or justice of the peace as soon as the woman is pregnant. Even in the past, when premarital sex was largely frowned upon, fathers didn't get out their shotguns to lead a prospective son-in-law to the altar until their daughter was pregnant, even though they almost certainly knew perfectly well what was going on between the young people. It is pregnancy that is the real sexual link with marriage, not intercourse.

Yet side by side with this widely held attitude toward procreation is the modern idea that the Ideal Wife is beautiful and totally husband-centered – always available to him, always responsive to his sexual needs and always sexually desirable. And the ideal of sexual desirability is immature; the perfect beauty of the 1970s is thin, narrow-hipped, flat-bellied and with small, firm, pink-nippled breasts. This is the way an adolescent girl looks, not the way a pregnant woman looks, nor is it, usually, the way a mother looks.

The effects of a first pregnancy on a young couple vary enormously, depending on so many variables that it is almost impossible to create any sort of stereotype. This does not alter the fact that there is a stereotype which is put across energetically in all forms of popular entertainment. The Little Wife tells her husband the great, glad news. He is at first amazed. Such an eventuality had never, of course, crossed his mind; he has at no point considered the link between intercourse and pregnancy, and naturally he has been totally unaware of his wife's missing periods for the past two months or so, or of any changes in her breasts.

His next reaction is delight. He fusses over her with great tenderness while she laughs indulgently, and he insists that she must rest and take care of her precious self.

For the next six months or so, we see the couple growing closer together and more loving, happily buying little rattles and potties (always potties! – the emphasis on correct toilet behavior starts early) until she goes into labor with a bang – sudden shriek of pain, grabbing of belly, doubling over in agony – and the cry goes out for hot water.

The reality is very different. First of all, it would be a very detached married man who was not as aware of his wife's menstrual cycle as she is. Whether or not they opt to desist from intercourse while she is menstruating, he will know when her periods are expected and therefore will suspect as soon as she does that a pregnancy has started.

In addition to the period changes, there are other physical changes, notably in breast size and sensitivity, and in nipple color; it would be an unusually unperceptive male who did not notice.

(Incidentally the popular stereotype regarding the onset of labor is equally wrong; it is, generally speaking, singularly lacking in drama, being little more than a dull and rather unglamorous backache. As for the hot water – as an ex-midwife I can't for the life of me imagine what it is supposed to be for, apart from providing employment for the onlookers or perhaps a pot of tea.)

There is no sudden Moment of Knowledge as there is in the stereotype. In fact there is a period of wondering, lasting as long as two months, which gradually hardens into certainty. The use of modern pregnancy tests, which can be performed when the first period is merely late, has shortened it.

If the couple have planned the baby, then the period of wondering is a hopeful, enjoyable one and may well bring the pair closer together. If it is an unplanned pregnancy and there has been a failure of contraception, the period is a fearful and unpleasant one and is very likely to drive a wedge between them.

Once the pregnancy is a *fait accompli*, attitudes continue to change. If it is a wanted child there is a time of euphoria, with the stereotyped preparations going on – redecorating a room to make it into a nursery, shopping for baby clothes and so on. However, if the couple are at all superstitious – and a great majority are – they may not start any preparations until the third month is past, for fear of miscarriage. There is a widespread belief, even among educated, sensible people, that getting ready for a baby too soon is a direct cause of miscarriage and stillbirth.

If the couple are unwillingly pregnant, the confirmation of the pregnancy may lead to discussion of the possibility of abortion. What happens to the pair who go ahead and dispose of a pregnancy in this way is another story. At this point let us go on to look at the situation of the unwillingly pregnant.

The period succeeding confirmation can be traumatic in the extreme, depending on which of the couple feels most strongly about the situation. A woman may be more able to accept the pregnancy than her husband (she's often biologically driven to do so, however much her intellect or surface emotions reject her state), and her attempts to protect her developing baby may enrage her less willing husband.

In the movie *New York, New York* is just such a case, with the couple splitting up once the baby is born because the father cannot accept the pressures that parenthood has put on him or the way it has deprived him of his wife's services. She gives up singing with his dance band on tour as soon as she is pregnant in favor of taking it easy in order to save the baby, and as a result of her absence he loses popularity and the band fails. He finds this dereliction on her part unforgivable.

If the husband is more eager for parenthood than his wife, the problems are exacerbated. She may suffer pregnancy symptoms to a severe degree – sickness, sleeplessness and general misery – to "punish" him for what he has done to her by making him see her agony. Or she may deliberately live it up, drinking too much, smoking too much and resting too little in order to threaten him by threatening the welfare of the pregnancy.

In the movie *Mr. Skeffington*, based on a novel of the same title, a beautiful and vivacious young woman (played by Bette Davis) marries an ugly, middle-aged man (played by Claude Rains), mainly in order to protect and help her scapegrace brother (see chapter 4 for a discussion of in-laws). When she becomes pregnant her husband is delighted, but she is appalled. She tries to spoil the pregnancy through her behavior but totally fails, and the fact that she is far more concerned about possible damage to her looks than about the baby causes him a great deal of pain.

A couple's sexual behavior during a pregnancy will clearly depend on which attitudes are present – pleasure or rejection. It will also depend on such factors as financial anxiety ("Can we afford a baby?"), maturity anxiety ("Are we capable of bringing up a child?") and fear of loss ("Will the baby spoil our lives/my looks/our freedom?").

For some couples pleasure in the pregnancy leads naturally to a great increase in sexual activity. Many newly pregnant couples report making love far more often than even during their honeymooning days. This can be due not only to shared pleasure in their incipient parenthood but can also be hormonal. Some women experience a great increase in sexual desire once they become pregnant, due to the change in their hormone balance as well as to psychological factors.

Knowing that you are a "complete woman," capable of conceiving, can make a woman feel so intensely feminine that her libido leaps to hitherto unreached heights. And not only is there nothing quite as aphrodisiac for any man as an eager sexual partner – her husband too feels a "complete man" because he has impregnated her successfully.

Dear Claire,

I am three months pregnant, and very happy about it, but I do wonder whether it is all right for me to feel as I do. I want to have sex so much, and I have two or three orgasms every time, which I don't usually do. Sometimes I even find myself masturbating when my husband isn't home, I get so urgent. Please tell me – can this harm the baby? Could it damage him in his development, or make him grow up to be a sex maniac?

For some couples happiness about the pregnancy can lead to *less* sex, especially if anxieties about the pregnancy's progress when the mother feels sexy are unexpressed and not dispelled. It is interesting how many parents-to-be express a fear of producing a child who will become a sexy adult as a direct result of their own sexuality. What would be so terrible about that?

Another obvious and common cause of less sex in early pregnancy is unpleasant symptoms in the mother. If she is sick a great deal she may regard bed as a place of rest and peace, not fun, and this can rebound unfortunately on a young husband. He may see her sickness more as a rejection of him rather than something due to hormonal imbalance – and he may well be right. Just as feeling like a completely feminine woman because of pregnancy can combine with the new hormonal state to create a great rise in libido, so the fear of even a wanted pregnancy, and anger directed at the cause of the pregnancy, can combine with the same hormones to create nausea, illness and loss of libido. As the pregnancy progresses these problems may be resolved – either by the couple coming to terms with the change in their circumstances and accepting it happily, or by their failure to make the adjustment and separating (as happened with the couple in *New York, New York*). The situation, may on the other hand, remain fairly static and not be resolved until after the child's birth.

At this point, however, let's look at the couple whose expectations are damaged, either by failure to conceive at all or by miscarriage. What effect does this have on their behavior?

Cathy and Donald married later in life than many of their friends – he was twenty-eight, she was twenty-five. Most of the people they knew of their own age already had two, three or even four children. He worked in advertising and had once been an actor. She was a hospital nurse. Before they married Don talked rather sentimentally about having children, seeing himself as a happy parent in a rose-tinted world. Cathy, working as she did in a children's hospital and having some experience of child care, was far less sanguine. Also, her own childhood had been unhappy and she had always said she "wouldn't risk hurting anyone as much" as her parents had hurt her, so she'd have no children. They couldn't afford children when they first married, anyway, and she was fitted with a diaphragm.

After two years of marriage she developed a menstrual irregularity that made them think that their contraception had failed, and after initial dismay on Cathy's part and some financial anxiety on Don's – they were far from well off, though they did own their own home – they came to terms with the situation. However, she miscarried, and because they had made a psychological adaptation to the idea of parenthood they decided to try to start another pregnancy, deliberately this time, even though their anxiety over the situation had damaged their sexual pleasure. Also, Cathy still had considerable reservations about having children – but none about being pregnant. *That* she now wanted, and wanted badly.

"It would be like carrying a bit of Don around with me. It would be an extra bit of us."

She did not conceive, however. After several months of false hopes because of delayed periods and what might have been very early miscarriages they made an appointment to attend a fertility clinic.

"Mad, really," Cathy says now. "In fact, I didn't want to have children – but I definitely wanted to have a successful pregnancy. I was thinking through two heads in a way. Anyway, my dander was up – dammit, any cow in a field could do it – but me, educated, capable, sensible me – I couldn't get pregnant. No way was I going to let fate get away with that."

They went through two years of complex hormone therapy (Cathy had had thyroid surgery as a girl, and this contributed to her fertility problem) and regular treatment for Don (who had a marginally low sperm count) all of it accompanied by considerable sexual tensions during which Cathy and Don both suffered a loss of libido. Finally, they had their first child, a daughter who was born prematurely. The early months of her care were difficult, but she thrived.

Once again Cathy showed signs of hormone imbalance, failing to menstruate for several months, and their doctor made a tentative diagnosis of another pregnancy. As a result they sold their apartment and moved to a larger house (which neither liked very much). But this again turned out to be a false alarm, and once more the couple attended a fertility clinic.

"I didn't mean to have another child so soon, but these damned failures – they made me so *angry*," Cathy said. They succeeded again and this time had a son, also born prematurely but healthy. He was a difficult though vigorous child, and both parents were exhausted by him. Cathy also suffered a fairly severe attack of postpartum depression after his birth.

They decided now that their family was complete, with one child of each sex, and resumed contraception. However, three years later, to their surprise, they had an "accident" – Cathy forgot to use her cap one night. Don, by this time disabused of his more romantic notions about parenthood, talked about an abortion – he didn't want another child. "Two kids are two kids, but three's a bloody army," he said. Cathy was not very happy about the idea – she enjoyed pregnancy enormously, usually feeling well and particularly sexy – but valued Don's peace of mind enough to be willing to go along with him. However, one day he said casually, "If it's a boy, let's call him Ambrose," and she knew he had come to terms with the pregnancy.

Now the three children are all teenagers and the family is affluent and happy, but both parents agree that they had their children for the wrong reasons.

"Subfertility and recurrent miscarriages made the whole thing into a battle between us and Providence – and we set out to win. It's a Pyrrhic victory in some ways. They're great children – but we don't really see ourselves as the right people to be parents. One thing that is very good, though – we are still more important to each other than the children are to us. If we had to choose the children would come second every time. We have a better marriage, we both think, than we might have had if we hadn't had to overcome our confused feelings about having children."

These two were fortunate in that when they picked up the challenge biology threw at them, they managed to win. Their success enriched their relationship. But for many people, failure to conceive or to successfully carry a pregnancy to term acts as a divisive force.

"As a clinical psychologist attached to a fertility clinic, I meet lots of couples, all tense, all anxious, all a bit on the defensive side when they first come. They're looking for someone or something to blame for their problem. They're ashamed to have it. Whose fault? Where did the doctor go wrong? Which of us is to blame? These are the questions they keep asking. My job is to try to help them see their situation as one that has to be accepted by both, that no one is ever to blame (though the religious ones floor me a bit by saying God is punishing them, and as an agnostic, I can't argue with them anyway they don't believe me). Then I have to help them to talk about what they'll do if the treatment we can offer doesn't succeed in giving them a baby. I used to tell them that we don't talk about failure or success – just babies, or no babies. I'd explain that every marriage can be successful and happy, with or without children – the important thing is to face up to the no-children possibility. I say to them, we can't even begin treatment in the physical sense until we've sorted this out. That, in fact, is what we tried to do. The gynecologist and the endocrinologist on our team were very good and very sure we were right in the design we'd made for the running of the unit, but after three years we had to admit defeat. Patients just aren't accessible to the sort of rearrangement of thinking we were trying to provide until after they know for sure they can't conceive. So, my job now is more remedial than preventive – I mean, I help with the couples who find their sex life is suffering, the men who prematurely ejaculate, the women who lose their libido and stop having orgasms – sometimes I find myself presiding at the divorce, almost. All because they can't conceive. Yet over and over these same people admit to me that they don't have strong feelings for children as such – that they don't especially like the company of other people's children. It's just that they want their own. And without their own, lots of them that stop caring for each other.

How much of this powerful drive comes from inside and how much from without? That a lot of it comes from outside – is exogenous – is undoubted. As we've already seen, the pressures on married people to conform to a childbearing norm are intense, so much so that a self-defensive organization, the National Organization of Non Parents (NON) was founded in the United States and the National Association of the Childfree in Great Britain. But this is not the only pressure. Powerful though outside forces are, internal or endogenous factors are even greater and cannot be ignored.

Women in particular often find themselves overtaken by an intense desire for a child, a desire so intense that they may, if thwarted, actually steal another woman's baby and try to pass it off as their own. Cases like this are commonplace and, probably inevitably, occur most often among women recovering from a miscarriage or the birth of a stillborn child. The biological drive to motherhood is exceedingly strong and can bewilder the most rational women with its intensity, since it can overwhelm carefully formulated and perfectly logical intellectual decisions not to reproduce. These pressures on a marriage are made much more complicated when one or the other partner has had a child by a previous relationship.

Dear Claire,

Mike has a daughter of seven, from his first marriage, and he sees her every week, even though I've been going to the fertility clinic for the past three years. If he really loved me, he'd understand my feelings and he wouldn't see the kid, would he?

Dear Claire,

I have had two children, and my husband loves them dearly, even though he knows that my relationship with their father was a very bad one. *He* refused to marry me, for a start. My husband feels very bad about the fact that we don't seem able to start another baby, but I tell him, he may not be a father, but he's a husband, and that makes up more than enough for what we're losing out of not having a child of our own. He doesn't believe me though, and I worry a lot because I can see it driving him away from me. He gets very moody about it.

Dear Claire,

Ever since my husband discovered that the reason we can't have a baby is that he has a subnormal sperm count, he has gone right off sex. If I dare say anything about it, he throws up in my face that I had an abortion when I was sixteen. We used to be happy, really, till this pregnancy thing got to us. I think it's ruining our marriage now.

In a way, having one partner to blame can create a curious sort of harmony in a childless marriage; it may not be the sort of relationship many people would find satisfactory, but if it works for the two people involved, that may be good enough.

Sam was a widower with two sons of five and seven when he married Alice, a very motherly young woman some fifteen years his junior. She was an excellent stepmother and reared the two boys very well, but she never had a child of her own. They saw doctors and it was discovered that the problem, far from being any reproductive inadequacy on Alice's part – which the couple had naturally enough assumed – was in fact due to disease in Sam. He had, in the first year of grief after his first wife's death, "run wild" with a number of prostitutes. He had picked up gonorrhea and as a result had suffered sufficient damage to the *vas deferens* (the sperm-carrying tubes) of both testicles to become virtually sterile, though he was still fully potent. Neither he nor the doctors ever told Alice the true cause of his infertility – they said simply that it was something that had happened to him after his two children had been conceived. Alice said she did not mind too much – she had the stepsons, after all – and the family seemed happy.

But over the years the balance of power in the family seemed to shift, until, by the time the boys had grown up and left home, Sam lived almost as a servant in his own home. He worked full time at his job as a railwayman, but in the morning he got up early and did all the housework, completing the chores when he returned in the evening. He bought the food in his lunch hour and cooked the evening meal. His weekends were devoted to the laundry, ironing and mending.

Alice did nothing. Nothing at all. She lay in bed most of the day, ate a great deal and became very fat. Sam's colleagues laughed at him, and he was a byword in his town for being so "henpecked and soft." But when Alice died suddenly of a stroke Sam was almost inconsolable. He told his church minister that he "couldn't live with" himself after the dreadful way he'd "made poor Alice suffer" – he'd "never be able to make it up to her now." He attempted suicide twice before being admitted to a mental hospital with severe depression and he has still not recovered.

Not all childless couples cope with their stress in the same way. Some turn on each other and become mutually destructive; the couple in Edward Albee's *Who's Afraid of Virginia Woolf?* tear each other apart throughout the play's agonizing couple of stage hours, and we find at the heart of their relationship a fantasy child, for they never had a real one. (There are also other complex overtones, of course, especially involving the relationship between the wife and her father.)

Some are able to use their hunger more constructively. Child care services from schools to hospitals, scout groups to orphanages, are often supported and staffed by devoted people who, lacking their own biological offspring, devote their lives to the care of other people's. James Hilton's eponymous character in the novel *Goodbye Mr. Chips* was based on a very real life sort of person.

But more important than the problems of the childless (if only because the childless are in the minority) are the problems suffered by women who bear the stigmata of motherhood. It is one of the great injustices of life that men carry a much lighter and more agreeable share of the reproductive burden than women. An average man who enjoys a modest degree of sexual activity over a reproductive lifetime starting around the age of fifteen could, if he managed to impregnate a woman with every ejaculation of his semen, father some eight thousand children without suffering any ill effects. Quite the reverse in fact. If he were a little more randy than usual he could raise the total to ten thousand without much effort. A woman, on the other hand, could produce only forty children (unless she consistently had twins or triplets) during her reproductive lifetime from, on average, age fifteen to fifty-five, and she would suffer markedly as a result, if she survived such a childbearing marathon. According to the *Guinness Book of Records* one woman actually produced 69 offspring in twenty-seven multiple pregnancies. But she is, after all, acknowledged as a recordholder.

The physical detriment she would suffer would be, first, to her skin, which stretches over the burgeoning breasts and belly during pregnancy. It may fail to regain its full elasticity afterward, leaving the woman with what are medically known as *striae*, wrinkled, purple-red lines fading to silvery gray or white, which can leave a once-smooth expanse of skin looking like a piece of crumpled paper. Stretch marks can cover the thighs and the upper arms as well as the belly and breasts. They are not pretty, though most male doctors do not consider them serious complaints. But then, men rarely suffer from *striae*.

Sagging breasts are also a common sequel to childbearing. It is probably a biological norm that the human breasts should be pendulous and empty and flat except during lactation; certainly many African and South American women from primitive tribes show this pattern in maturity. For Western women, however, reared to regard breasts primarily as sexual toys for their partners and as embellishments to be admired, rather than as functional glands to be used for feeding purposes, such a change from the virginal small, up-turned breast of girlhood can be demoralizing.

Another physical change which is less immediately apparent, but of which the woman and her sexual partner may be all too aware, is loss of tone in the muscles of the vagina and the pelvic floor. This can lead to a "baggy" vagina. Usually the vagina is a potential tube – that is, its walls are touching each other, rather like an empty toothpaste tube. It can then stretch a great deal when necessary to accommodate either an erect penis, or the skull of a full term infant. But the tension of the muscles of the vaginal walls adds sensation to intercourse for both the woman and her partner, and if that tension is lost because of overstretching during childbirth the loss of sexual satisfaction can be considerable.

If there is added to this such weakness of the pelvic floor that a cough, sneeze or laugh can cause the bladder to expel some of its contents, since the sphincter – or ring – muscle that guards the outlet is similarly weakened; if there are hemorrhoids or an anal fissure at the opening of the rectum; this can add greatly to the woman's discomfort, both physical and psychological. Few of us can accept with equanimity the fact that an unexpected sneeze can result in underwear that is wet, possibly smelling of urine, and skin that is painfully rubbed by the dampness.

That motherhood can do this to a woman and make her both be and feel less desirable as a sexual partner is a fact that many women contemplate with bitterness, especially as it does not happen to all. A great many mothers totally escape being marked by their childbearing, and they are lucky. It *is* more luck than judgment. It is supposed to be more "mature" to be able to tolerate such physical changes in exchange for the so-called joys of parenthood. It is thought to be mere "vanity" to feel reluctant to display one's bare skin on a beach because of the pleated effect of stretch marks. It is supposed to be "childish" to want up-standing breasts rather than empty bean bags.

Possibly all this is true – but in a society which puts an inordinate amount of value on a woman's sexual desirability, and which seems to despise older women entirely because they are older so that hiding one's age once one passes the thirty mark becomes almost required, it is hardly just to blame women for feeling as they do about the mess motherhood may make of them. *Especially as all too often their men feel the same about it.* Many are the marriages that end in divorce courts because "she isn't the girl I married any more." It is ludicrous for any man to expect that he can acquire a wife, make her a mother, and still keep her as a girl, but too many of them do expect it. The joke about "trading in a forty-year-old wife for a couple of nice new twenties" isn't really that funny – too many men actually try it.

This is one area, of course, in which childlessness pays big dividends. There can be little doubt that a woman who has never had a child retains a younger-looking figure and skin longer than her fecund sister. In addition, she has never "damaged" her sexuality in her partner's eyes by giving birth. The man who has actually seen a baby pushed out of the vagina that provides him with his sexual satisfaction may find it difficult to regard that vagina's owner in quite the same light as he once did. The man who has never had to share his wife's body with his offspring suffers less confusion about her sexual attractiveness. On the other hand, men with a strong drive to fatherhood may feel a childless wife is less feminine than a fertile one and may react accordingly. Sometimes such a man will cast himself as the child of the marriage and treat his wife more as a mother; sometimes he will cast his wife in the child role and "father" her.

Either way, the childless couple can go on together for many years with little to spoil the even tenor of their sexual ways. Boredom may crop up, of course, but not the jealousy of one child, or partiality for another, that almost inevitably occurs in marriages which have produced children. These definitely do affect parents and their children, of course.

6
Mothers and Sons

HUMAN BEINGS ARE ALWAYS either male or female
(apart from the very rare individuals who are born with
the congenital abnormality of hermaphroditism) yet,
oddly, in many languages the word for a newborn
human is neuter in gender – the baby, *das kind*, *nene*.
The words used imply that people regard the newborn
person, whatever its genitals are, as a totally non-
sexual creature.

Yet this is absurd; the baby girl already has in her
small ovaries her full complement of ova, unripe of
course, but ready and waiting for their season. The
baby boy already has the basic equipment he will need
to produce millions of sperm when his time comes. Both
have had this firm stamp of sexuality from the moment
of conception, and by the eleventh week of intrauterine
life the necessary organs have developed to prove it.

The denial of the new baby's sex underlines just how
important gender actually is. Individual parents as well
as the social groups to which they belong care a great
deal about the gender of their child; almost the first
question a new mother asks is "what is it?" (actually
the *very* first is "is it all right?") and the birth is usually
announced in terms of gender. ("It's a boy!")

And from birth onward the mother reacts to her
child in different ways, depending on the child's
gender. The way she handles it, talks to it, feeds it,

trains it and expects it to behave will be governed by her view of what "masculinity" and "femininity" are or should be.

In countries where the old traditions prevail, mothers have few problems. Girls are dressed in pink and boys in blue, boys are given more food than girls, boys are allowed to be noisier than girls, girls are allowed to cry more than boys, girls are allowed to show more fears than boys and so on. However, in countries where political ideas about gender differences are very important at the moment, it's rather tougher. A modern woman, who has absorbed from her childhood experiences of her own mother's attitudes beliefs about gender differences, and who tries to graft on to this her newfound views on sexual equality and the importance of nonsexist methods of child care, can get very bogged down in the resulting confusion.

Patty gave birth to her first child, Alex, when she was thirty. A native New Yorker, she had married an English writer whom she met during her work as a publisher's editor, and they had remained in New York after the ceremony. Very articulate, informed, and a staunch supporter of the Women's Movement, she had always said that any child she had would be reared as a *person*, not as a "boy" or "girl." Her husband was totally supportive in this, and made it clear that he would not in any way interfere with these plans. Not for him the "male chauvinist" attitude of trying to imprint his child with false notions of masculinity.

To Patty's distress, breast-feeding failed (she had a severe breast abscess), but since she was also a strong proponent of "natural" lifestyles, she persisted longer than most women would have. However, she had to admit defeat when Alex was ten days old, after which he was established satisfactorily on a bottle.

She attended an infant clinic in her neighborhood and received excellent support from the pediatrician there. He noted that she seemed distressed and tense, but put this down to a combination of her sense of loss over the breast-feeding failure combined with a mild degree of postpartum depression. However, as the weeks went on Alex failed to thrive. His weight remained low and he was fretful and difficult. Patty said he cried a great deal, and she was almost at the end of her tether.

It was decided to admit Alex and his mother to the hospital for observation, and Patty was asked to bring her own feeding equipment and to feed him exactly as she did at home. The nurse reported after two days that the problem was clear: Alex was being badly underfed. In fact, the baby was almost starving.

The nurse also reported to the doctor that when she had said gently to Patty, "I think he needs more food – he's a big hungry boy with a lot of growing to do," she lost her temper and for the first time was rude and unpleasant.

The doctor talked to Patty at length and at last the situation became clear: she was worried about the risk of overfeeding her baby. Everything she had ever read about obesity made the point that the problem of obesity often started in infancy. This was why she was particularly upset at her failure to breast-feed, because the books had also said that "breast-fed babies cannot be overfed." Having had to settle for the bottle, she wasn't going to fall into the trap of giving the baby too much, and above all, she was going to avoid the even worse trap of thinking boys needed more food than girls. Her best friend's baby, who was a girl, was thriving on the same quantities of food she was giving Alex.

It took time and a lot of encouragement to help

Patty see that in satisfying her baby's appetite she was not "pandering to stereotypes of masculinity" but was observing his needs as a *person*, and that what suited one child did not necessarily suit another. The fact that her friend's child needed less food was due not to her gender but to her constitution. She was helped to realize that she had been discriminating against her own child on the grounds of his gender; had he been a girl, Patty would have fed her according to her needs rather than according to her own theories.

Now, at the age of three-and-a-half, Alex seems physically well but does show some signs of emotional difficulty. In particular he is very aggressive toward other children at his nursery school. His teachers think this could be due to the fact that his mother strongly discourages any show of aggression at home. Also the parent's marriage is somewhat strained, and Patty complains that she is being "relegated to mere maternity and domesticity." The future of the family looks rather bleak at present.

The attempt to deny that there are differences between boys and girls right from birth is one of the more unfortunate aspects of the cultural and political movements toward sexual equality. Of course, it is high time that the uglier manifestations of sexism were swept away, but a denial of reality is not the way to do it. Surely, equality depends on recognizing differences and creating a flexible society within which these can be accommodated without injustice to anyone, rather than attempting to impose an artificial standard of sameness.

Of course not every mother holds political and social views so strong that they consciously affect the way she handles and relates to her child. For the majority of us the drives that mold our behavior come up from well below the level of consciousness, political or otherwise.

A woman reared to regard males automatically as more important, more powerful, more intelligent, more everything than she is, and to run her life contentedly enough by deferring to the men in it, may be very tentative in her dealings with a son. There is a long tradition of mothers spoiling their sons more than their daughters, and many in the Women's Movement complain bitterly about the feminine "fifth column" who persist in rearing girls to be domestic and helpful at all times while allowing boys to grow up without ever expecting them to take on domestic responsibilities at all. They see it as going hand in hand with the idea that girls do not need education as boys do because they'll just get married.

But, in fact, the two ideas are separate. Mothers who see education as wasted on girls who will grow up to be mere domestic slaves like themselves do not encourage boys to be lazy at the expense of girls, simply because domestic jobs "naturally" belong to girls. Instead, it is often because the mother cannot command the authority to make her son do anything he does not particularly want to do. From birth she approaches her small boy in a spirit of subservience, just as she approaches her husband. They are both males, and though one is small and patently lacking in power, the power is there in him because he is male. Dormant, but *there*.

A possible clue to the way some mothers respond as they do to a boy baby is the fact that the newborn male's genitals are, in relation to the rest of his body, rather large. They may be swollen as a result of the effect of the mother's own hormones which are still circulating within him, and this can add to the effect of aggressive masculinity. Girls, too, may have swollen genitals, but enlarged *labia majora* do not dominate a baby's anatomy to the same degree.

If a woman gives birth to a daughter first, she may find that she copes better with learning the tasks and skills of mothering an infant. In a survey made in a prenatal clinic among women expecting their first babies (and therefore with no experience of child care on which to draw), more than half said they wanted a girl because "they're easier;" "they're smaller and the birth is easier;" "they settle to feeding more easily;" or "it's nicer having a girl first, they can help with the other babies later on."

These opinions were also given by mothers who had already had babies and were expecting their second or subsequent births – the only difference shown was that *more* of these mothers thought having a girl first was better. In both groups, incidentally, almost all the husbands were hoping for a boy.

It is interesting that so many mothers still believe that girls are "easier" to give birth to and to rear, "easier" feeders and better sleepers – because there is not a shred of hard evidence to suggest that this is so. Girls statistically are marginally lighter at birth than boys, but it is a small difference and far from being the rule. Plenty of girls hit the birth scales at over eight pounds, plenty of boys well below. Nor is there any evidence that giving birth to a girl is easier. But still mothers believe it – just as they tend to believe that a stormy pregnancy means they are carrying a boy, a peaceful one a girl. Clearly, beliefs like this tell us much more about mothers' attitudes to the gender of a baby than about what actually happens during pregnancy.

So a baby's place in the family can have an effect on the way a mother handles a child, just as much as can gender.

Marie gave birth to her first child, a daughter, in a very small, friendly hospital and breast-fed her successfully from the start, weaning her at the age of eight months. She and Debbie had a close relationship from the beginning, and when she was three Marie and her husband Danny decided to have another baby.

"It was a mixed-up sort of pregnancy. Sometimes I felt marvelous, just as I did when I was carrying Debbie, but at others I felt really ill, and would have to lie down for hours so as not to be sick. Debbie was great. She'd sit there beside me on the bed and stroke my hand and be so good and lovely – she was just like a real friend. When I felt well we enjoyed getting ready, Debbie and I. I told her right from the start, of course, and she's so bright, she understood very well, and would listen to my tummy 'to hear the baby,' she said. We'd go shopping together to buy clothes, and we washed and ironed all her own baby clothes ready for the new one and got the baby basket and crib ready – it was fantastic."

The birth should have happened at home – that was the plan – but there was a good deal of anxiety because the baby seemed distressed and Marie was rushed to a big general hospital for a forceps delivery. She was particularly upset at being parted from Debbie because she had wanted her to see the new baby as a welcome addition to the family rather than someone who took Mommy away. So when the child, a boy, was born, Marie felt less elated than she had at Debbie's birth.

Breast-feeding failed this time; she tried, but the baby fought at the breast, and Marie became very upset. The pediatrician advised bottle feeding, to which the baby took very well. Marie and the baby – the family called him Joel after Marie's dead father – returned home on the seventh day after the birth.

Debbie did not seem too disturbed by her mother's absence. There had been unlimited visiting at the hospital, and Marie spent all the time she could with her, allowing her to touch and handle Joel as much as possible. Marie looked forward to settling down quickly for she was an experienced mother and was sure she could manage well. Danny could only give a certain amount of support because of his work as a traveling salesman and though his company arranged for him not to go too far away from home for a few weeks, still he had a lot of ground to cover, and rarely reached home in the evening much before eight, when the children were in bed and left again at seven in the morning.

Debbie suddenly became ill when Joel was about two months old. She had a cold and then a series of fevers, aches and pains, and she was listless and unhappy. Marie became almost hysterical with anxiety. She was convinced that Debbie had leukemia, and though her doctor disagreed and thought it was simply a virus infection, she insisted on sending her into the hospital.

The results of a blood test were rather ambiguous, showing an altered white cell count that could have been due to a generalized infection. However, Marie became even more frantic when she heard. To ensure her peace of mind as well as because Debbie was still obviously ill, the pediatrician agreed to admit her for a series of tests.

Marie asked to be admitted with her as she was still under five, and the hospital agreed and said they could also accept Joel, by putting a crib in the cubicle with Debbie. This Marie refused. She said the baby cried too much and made Debbie lose her rest. Joel could go to her mother to be cared for – wasn't it a good thing she wasn't breast-feeding him, after all? – leaving Marie to look after Debbie who, she said, needed her most.

Debbie was in the hospital for several weeks, because there were puzzling aspects to the test results. Her temperature fluctuated wildly, and she was often lethargic and fretful. However, her blood tests offered no clue. The doctors were puzzled and watched carefully. Marie was a marvelous nurse to Debbie – always patient, alert and cheerful. The nurses liked her and appreciated her help, for she would make Debbie's bed, feed her, take her to the toilet, take her temperature, and so on.

During this time she showed no anxiety about Joel, saying her mother could look after him perfectly. "Especially as I have three brothers," she added, laughing. She never asked to leave the hospital to visit him or asked for him to be brought to her, but was content to accept news of him from her husband when he came to visit.

After six weeks the children's ward nurses were instructed to watch Marie more closely than they had; the doctors were suspicious about the ambiguities in Debbie's test results. The nurses reported that Marie had been manipulating Debbie's thermometer to give high readings. She had also been giving her the tranquilizers she herself had been prescribed for her tension over Debbie's illness. Hence the child's lethargy.

When confronted by the doctors Marie was first angry and denied any such behavior. She than broke down in great distress. She *had* been doing as they said – but it was because she knew Debbie wasn't well, and somehow she had to make sure she stayed in the hospital until the doctors found out what was really wrong.

A psychiatrist spent some time with Marie, and his analysis was that she could not cope with Joel and was attempting to return Debbie to infancy in his place. One phrase she had used had been illuminating: "I hate changing Joel's diapers. All those horrible bits and pieces – I can't feel comfortable handling him. And he keeps getting erections when I take the diaper off. It's horrible in a baby – yes, I know it's normal, but that doesn't stop it from being horrible."

When a child reaches what has been labeled the "age of negativism" or "toddler rebellion" at about the age of two, a mother needs to marshall a good deal of patience and understanding to ensure that both she and her child weather this stage with the minimum of stress. Not easy when the child's response to everything is a firm "No," perhaps accompanied by temper tantrums, and when being obstructive, awkward, trouble-seeking and generally hell to live with seems to be his or her sole ambition. And one that is far from being difficult to attain.

If the child is the son of a submissive woman, she may have considerable difficulty holding her own in the inevitable battles between them. It is often at this stage that the rot really sets in as far as sexist attitudes are concerned, and it sometimes lasts for life. A little boy of two or three who finds that his mother does not ever enforce her will but allows him to get away with whatever he wants, and whose only resource when she is driven too far is to bring father in ("See what you can do with him – he'll listen to you, but I can't get anywhere") is, by the time he is five, well-primed with machismo. It may not flower in all its glory for several years yet, but it is a sturdy little growth for all that.

Sometimes the opposite situation can develop. A woman who is resentful of her subservient position vis-a-vis men, and who has always at some deep level resented the power exerted by father, brothers and husband, may see in a small child an object of masculinity which she can safely dominate, just as masculinity has always dominated her. Once again, the way she behaves at this stage can govern the way the man (of whom the child is the father) behaves for the rest of his life.

One of the most successful – and funniest – situation comedy shows on British television some years ago was called *Me Mammy*. It chronicled the exploits of a Catholic bachelor, aged vaguely fortyish, and his frightful, domineering, man-hating mother. The comedy was derived less from the stereotype of the superstitious and rather hypocritical form of catholicism the mother practised, and her son's half-hearted attempts to deny his belief in them, as from her ball-crushing control of every aspect of her son's life. He was required to come home dead on time and to be ready to eat the food she had chosen to prepare for him whether he wanted it or not, while she sat, glittering-eyed, and watched him eat it forkful by forkful. He had to be ready to do what she wanted, go where she wanted, as soon as she wanted. All of which, while possibly reasonable in the mother of a four-year-old, is far from reasonable in the mother of a forty-year-old.

Much of the humor of the show came from watching this grown man try to wriggle his way out from under the burden of her mothering, especially from seeing him try to have some sort of sex life. Girls were anathema to his mother but not as bad as the hateful men who preyed on them. *Her* problem was continuing to see her son as the little, asexual boy whom she could bully and control, inside the skin of a frightened, desperately randy and already running-to-seed specimen of the much-hated "Man." *His* problem was to get what he wanted as a man while still basking in the comforts of being controlled, protected and coddled by a specimen of what he most feared and desired "Woman." While most audiences laughed loudly at the resulting contortions – and they were genuinely funny

– dismissing the caricatures with the comfortable thought, "Well, of course, it's nothing like real life," many viewers were well aware that though the portraits painted were verging on caricature, they were drawn unerringly from life.

There is yet another way a woman who is uneasy in her dealings with men may build a relationship with her masculine child – by using him as a surrogate partner. Many are the women who "married" their baby sons on the day they gave them birth.

Bridie was the oldest daughter of a Catholic family of nine children, and she had always said she wanted only to marry and have children of her own. At the age of seventeen she married her first boyfriend, Michael, a long-haul truck driver some five years her senior. She moved in with him and his widowed mother. The first year was stormy: Bridie and her mother-in-law hated each other from the start and fought over who should look after Michael. Bridie told Michael they couldn't have a normal sex life while his mother was in the apartment because she "just couldn't. It wouldn't be right." Michael, a peaceable young man, gave in to the pressure, and after much drama his mother was shipped off to live with her sister in the South of Ireland.

Bridie, now aged eighteen, became pregnant almost as soon as her mother-in-law had gone. She gave birth to a daughter, Ann, and the following year she had another daughter, Maggie. Then she had three miscarriages in succession, over which she mourned a great deal. The family moved to a larger flat when she became pregnant again, when Ann was five and Maggie four.

She gave birth to a son, Gary, after a very stormy and lengthy labor. She had needed five pints of blood because of a postpartum hemorrhage. The baby was big –

over ten pounds in weight – and slow to breathe, but after a worrying twenty-four hours he was said by the doctors to be in "satisfactory" condition.

Bridie took him home at the age of ten days and there was a big family party, with all Bridie's relatives invited, for the christening. A first son was a very special event, she said. The baby cried throughout the ceremony and at the party, and Michael, who was rather drunk by halfway through the day, told Bridie's mother: "That boy'll never be any good, you mark my words. All this fuss . . . He'll bring nothing but trouble on our heads, just you wait and see."

That night he tried to have intercourse with Bridie who refused, claiming she still felt pain from her stitches. Michael, now even more drunk, lost his temper and hit her. The little girls woke up and scream-ed blue murder, and neighbors called the police. The next morning Michael was very ashamed of himself, very distressed and promised Bridie he would never lay a finger on her again, and the family settled down to a more peaceful life.

Bridie was clearly very proud of her family, especially her son. He was a demanding baby and often vomited, and the pediatrician said she thought he was being overfed. Bridie strongly disagreed and went on giving him extra-strength bottle feedings.

She went to the hospital for her postnatal checkup when Gary was eight weeks old and told Michael the doctor had said she wasn't to be "bothered with sex" for three months. Michael unhappily accepted the stipulation and began to work longer hours, which suited Bridie well as she needed extra money for the children.

Gary went on being a demanding, difficult baby, but Bridie seemed to cope well enough, accepting the need to concentrate on him as inevitable. The little girls,

Ann and Maggie, spent more time during the week with their maternal grandmother. When Michael was home between driving jobs he would take them out of Bridie's way to give her "the chance to catch up" with herself, and this the little girls enjoyed hugely.

By the time Gary was three he was known by the neighbors as "a little monkey," being big, hard to control and rather aggressive, who was liable to beat up other children with whom he was left to play. The parish priest came to see his mother. Why, he wanted to know, were there no more babies on the horizon? To see so young a Catholic mother – Bridie was by now twenty-seven – with only three children saddened him. Bridie made it immediately clear that there was nothing sinful going on; "But the doctor said I had such a bad time before, with my Gary, that I wasn't to be put through it again for a long time, if ever, and Michael is a good man. Some men wouldn't listen, but not Michael. He's a good man."

The priest seemed satisfied and went away, and life went on much as usual, with Michael spending most of the week away from home on long hauls, and his weekends with his little girls. Gary grew bigger and noisier. The girls spent a lot of their time after school helping Bridie and the apartment was kept spotless. The whole family went to church regularly every Sunday, met the in-laws – Bridie's ever-enlarging family of nieces and nephews, her sisters and brothers, and, of course, her mother. Aside from the arguments with neighbors over Gary's fighting and the occasional episodes of vandalism of which he was accused, all was well.

Then Gary, aged eleven, was brought home by the police one night, having been caught breaking into a local store. It was one of the rare evenings when Michael was home, and he hit the roof. In his rage he took off his belt and beat Gary hard – clearly to the policeman's approval. Bridie, who had been at her sick mother's came home in the middle and almost went berserk, attacking Michael and having to be physically restrained by the policeman.

The family appeared in the family court when Gary was brought there for the crime for which he had been arrested. Bridie, in great distress, assured them that he was a "good boy, never caused any trouble with anyone, just a high-spirited lad. Boys will be boys." When the story of Michael's beating of the child was told, and his bruises seen, it was decided it would be better for the boy if he were sent away to a reform school for a year. Bridie had hysterics when she heard this, accused Michael of being to blame, "because you've always been jealous of my Gary," and again tried to attack him. She had to be sedated by a police doctor, and was admitted as an emergency to a psychiatric hospital, because she was so out of control. Michael had to stay at home with sixteen-year-old Ann and fifteen-year-old Maggie, because Bridie had to stay in hospital for a month. During this time, Bridie's mother died, and she relapsed into uncontrollable rage again, blaming Michael for this as well. If he hadn't treated Gary so badly, her son wouldn't have been sent away, and Gary being sent away was what killed her mother. Michael said nothing. He became deeply depressed and both his daughters were very worried about him.

Presented in this inevitably shortened format, the emotions and needs that governed the relationship between Bridie, her son and her husband are clear. Michael's potency was threatened from the very start of his marriage by his mother's presence, which Bridie saw as an intrusion into her marriage and a threat to her own sexual expression. Not until he sent his mother away could he enjoy normal sex, and as a staunch

Catholic there was no other way he could get licit sex except within marriage. That there must have been guilt attached to his sexual satisfaction is obvious – since he was only able to obtain it at the expense of his mother's happiness. When his son was born, giving Bridie such a "bad time" guilt once again reared its head, showing itself to an extent in his rejection of his infant son ("He'll bring nothing but trouble on our heads") and compounded by his loss of control when Bridie refused him sex and he hit her. Even before the boy was a year old Michael had ceded the field to him. The boy was the center of Bridie's life, the source of all her satisfaction, just as Michael himself had been to his own mother. Clearly Gary was the sort of male figure Bridie admired – rough, aggressive and noisy, the antithesis of the usually quiet Michael. Her husband's only function, for Bridie, had been to provide the male partner she *most* desired.

The next important transition stage in the relationship between a mother and a son comes as the boy enters puberty, and so more obviously displays his masculinity, but before considering the effects this has, it is important to look at the other major relationship in a growing boy's life – the one he has with his father.

7
Fathers and Sons

"It's VERY EASY TO become a father – very hard to be one," goes the old adage, and like most of those tiresome old saws it is dripping with truth.

For a man, the act of creating a new human being is one of unalloyed pleasure. Sexual intercourse culminating in orgasm with ejaculation is the be-all and end-all of a man's reproductive life. Not for him the tedium of forty weeks of a gradually increasing burden in his belly accompanied by assorted side-effects ranging from nausea and vomiting to backache and back again. Not for him the effortful expulsion of the birth followed by months of feeling like a dairy. It is this fact that probably lies behind much of that feminine anger against men which is currently having a great deal of public expression; and heaven knows it is justifiable. Even if irremediable.

That men suffer guilt about the burden they lay on women is undoubted. It is expressed in the popular stereotype of the father-to-be fussing over his pregnant wife; it is expressed in the uneasy jokes men make about pregnancy ("leaving a bun in the oven"; "putting her in the club"), and the other most important stereotype – of the father waiting outside the labor ward. There he is, wreathed in cigarette smoke, marching up and down in deep anxiety, with his hair bedraggled, his face twisted with anxiety, and his hands shaking with worry. He has to be seen to be suffering, seen to be going through some sort of painful experience to match that being suffered by the woman on the other side of the door, who was put there by his "selfish" action.

And of course the other great stereotype that has been born of men's guilt about the inequality of reproduction is the "boy's best friend is his mother" one. It ranges widely, from gooey birthday cards trimmed with tinsel to the celebration of Mother's Day; from Al Jolson in *The Jazz Singer* crooning "Mammy" to his gray-haired old Mama (looking old enough to be his grandmother, actually), via songs like "My Yiddisher Momma" and "Mother Machree," to figures of the Madonna and child in Renaissance paintings. And it has been turned on its head by the American slang term of abuse "motherfucker," or "mother" for short. Just about the greatest insult one man can pay another is to call him a mother, so powerful is the stereotypical view of what a boy's mother ought to be.

In the past (and still today among some primitive peoples) men actually put themselves through a symbolic pregnancy and labor, delivering themselves of a rock – the practice of couvade – partly to deflect "evil spirits" from the vulnerable woman, but partly to expiate their own guilt. Such guilt, whether recognized and expressed or denied and repressed, inevitably lies behind a man's response to his newborn infant, whatever its gender – but there will be other responses which are very much due to the infant's gender, some of them obvious, others less so.

For example, many men take far more pleasure in having fathered a son than a daughter. They say so, loud and clear, and so common is the masculine desire for a child of his own gender that often everyone (women as well as men) takes it for granted that a man whose wife has produced a daughter is rather disappointed. The response to the birth of a first son, however far down the family he may come, tends to be a reaction more usual for a firstborn.

"When my son was born, after we'd had three daughters, everyone at the office slapped me on the back, made a great fuss of me, said things like 'made it at last' and 'high time you got yourself some backup at home' and 'thank God – you can shut up shop now' and things like that. I was furious. I mean I'd have been just as pleased with our new baby if it had been another girl. The way all these fellas assumed that the only reason we had four kids was because we'd been trying to have a boy every time made me want to spit. I told them, it takes a real man to have daughters – that I got no special charge out of having a son, and we'd probably have another baby just so we could get another daughter – they thought I was mad."

The male desire for sons is worldwide but is much greater in some cultures than others. It has been some time since girl babies were left exposed at the side of the road to die, because they were not worth the effort of rearing, but there remain overtones of the attitude in the way girls are reared in many societies – and the impetus toward male worship is always from the men themselves. Women may collude in it and allow themselves to feel like failures if they produce daughters instead of sons, but it is the male hunger for a creature of his own kind that leads the way.

And once more a popular stereotype lifts its head – the image of the elated new father handing out cigars as he announces the birth of a son. How Freudian can you get? Phallus-shaped objects to celebrate using a phallus to produce a child with a phallus of his own.

108 RELATED TO SEX

Why? What is it about reproducing himself, penis and all, that matters so much to so many men? Both sons and daughters carry the man's genes; both are the fruit of his loins in equal measure. Why should one kind of new human being be more highly regarded than the other?

I can think of several reasons. The first two are based on the way Western society structures its families. We live in what is essentially a patriarchy; it is the men who are seen as holders of power and riches, and it is they who identify the tribe. That is, the man's name is passed on to the new child. Some sporadic attempts are made to keep the mother's original family name going – that is, *her* father's – by giving it to the new child as a middle name. But, generally speaking, the baby of John Smith and Mary Smith (née Brown) will be named Jack Smith. So, the man who produces a son knows he has a chance of passing his own name on to yet another generation. This child will not, unlike a daughter, submerge his identity in another man's at marriage.

This is very important, for even in these sophisticated times there is magic in a name. Ancient peoples believed that knowledge of a man's true name gave power over him, and they would often keep the name of a person as a deep secret, using nicknames or false ones for normal use. Gods were often regarded as unnameable – the Jewish Jahveh (Jehovah) was one that could not be said. The word *"Adenoi"* – our Lord – would be used instead to address the deity. And, of course, swearing and other forceful forms of speech often involve using the name of the deity in a "wrong" way, just as many slang terms derive from this rather mystical attitude to names: "for Pete's sake" and "for the love of Mike" (both deriving from the names of angels); the French *nom d'un nom*; *sacre nom d'un chien* and so on. So, having a baby who will carry your name *all* his life is the cause of great rejoicing for a man.

This patriarchal system leads to the next important value of a male child – possessions. These, of course, can be passed on to either a son or a daughter, but daughters make bad custodians. In a very few years after their birth, they marry another man and take with them to his house their possessions – mostly derived from their father. Sons, on the other hand, not only keep their father's possessions in the family – when they marry they pull into the family net another man's possessions via his daughter. This is the system which underpinned for centuries the marriage practices of Europe as well as its politics. Royal and dynastic marriages shaped and reshaped the maps of that continent for a very long time.

Although the average man-in-the-street in the last third of the twentieth century may have little in the way of landed property or titles to pass on apart from a mortgaged home, and is unlikely in the extreme to need a fat dowry with which to marry off his daughter (or to be able to look forward to getting one via his son when *he* marries) still the old feelings linger. Sons are a better bet than daughters.

These are the more concrete of the reasons for welcoming a son – the others are less so, and may not be perceived by the man himself at a conscious level. For example, the guilt that a caring man may suffer because of the effort and pain his wife goes through to produce a child for him may make him welcome a son with relief. *This* child will not grow into an adult who will have to go through the pangs of childbirth.

But more important than that is the sense of identity a man has with a creature of his own gender. It is absurd to assume that an 8-lb scrap of humanity is a natural ally and friend of a 170-lb adult, yet this is the assumption made even if it is not directly expressed. He'll be someone to go to football matches with, someone to go camping and hunting with, or whatever.

The women's movement has been shouting its rage for many years about the way children are conditioned into assuming traditional male and female roles, and therefore has been attempting to change school teaching methods and eradicate from popular children's shows and books these stereotyped images. But the conditioning has already been started long before a child reaches the stage of being influenced by such things as school and entertainment. From the moment of birth, the parents' assumptions operate to mold the child's interests – and most particularly so when it comes to a man's son.

> "My boy Bill, I will see that he's named after me,
>   I will.
> My boy Bill, he'll be tall and as tough as a tree,
>   will Bill.
> Like a tree he'll grow with his head held high and
>   his feet planted firm on the ground,
> And you won't see nobody dare to try to boss him
>   or toss him around.
> No fat-bellied baggy-eyed bully will boss him
>   around."

The idea that between father and son there will be a community of interest stems from the irrational belief that males carry certain learned attitudes in their genes. No one will doubt that men and women are different, that women tend to be physically smaller than men and have a biological drive to be tender and nurturing in certain circumstances, while men have a biological drive to be aggressive and territorial in certain circumstances. But that doesn't mean that boy babies carry in their genes a taste for football, or that girl babies are born with dusters in their hands (although it cannot be denied that careful research has shown that males have superior visio-spatial abilities – they can throw things and assess distances more accurately – and also to have superior numerical reasoning ability, gross motor skills and mechanical aptitude, while females have greater verbal skills and better memories).

In fact this idea can lead to all sorts of tensions between the man and his son in later life (just as it can between a woman and her daughter). The man who wanted to be an engineer but had to become a furniture salesman to earn a living, and who likes jazz, hates rock and roll, enjoys hunting and ball games but despises indoor activities, will be first bewildered and then angry if, despite his attempts to extract these same ambitions and interests from deep inside his son where he believes they must lie dormant, the boy shows clearly that he wants no part of any of it. He's going to be a painter who likes classical music, is revolted by hunting and regularly plays chess and sits by the fire with a book. Such a father faced with such a son may in fact be convinced on the evidence of these "perverted" tastes that his son is "poofter" or "faggot" or whatever other delicate phrase for homosexual happens to be in use among his peers. He feels that no man who eschews "normal" manly interests can be a man – he must be de-sexed in some way.

But this lies in the future, of course, when a man first celebrates the birth of an infant son. It will be a long time before the problem of the boy's sexuality rears its head.

Or will it?

Ray and Jan had been married for about eight years

when he had a "nervous breakdown." He became very agitated and depressed and nearly lost his job as a result (he was a sales manager for a California wine producer). He was told that he needed hospital treatment, which he refused, but he agreed instead to have an hour's psychotherapy every week, together with drug treatment. During this psychotherapy, which went on for nine months, he was able to express a good deal of the emotion and anxiety he had been suppressing.

His mother had died when he was eight and his father, never a particularly affectionate man, had become very withdrawn from the boy. A series of half-hearted daily maids had been responsible for his care until he was about thirteen and considered old enough to fend for himself. He had been a consistent failure at school, to his father's disgust (he was a biochemist) and had finished high school at sixteen with no particular qualifications. He had drifted through a few jobs before settling comfortably with the wine firm; he enjoyed the traveling involved, and they provided him with a car. By this time he had left his father's home and had hardly any contact with him.

He had met Jan when he was twenty-one. She was then a school teacher and aged twenty-six – an age difference which worried her but not him. Their courtship was rather stormy as she resisted him because of the age difference, but after a year they married and bought a house. She went on teaching until Ray was promoted to sales manager, when he did not have to travel so much and earned more so that they felt they could afford a baby. Ray was not as enthusiastic about parenthood as Jan, but she was then twenty-nine and felt "time was running out." Ray agreed to the baby for Jan's sake. He made no bones about it: he told the therapist that for him the sun rose and set in Jan. His love for her was "overwhelmingly the most important thing that had ever happened to me. Not being with her was misery. I need her so much I used to get frightened by it."

During her pregnancy she was very sick and Ray became deeply anxious as well as very tense. For about four months she felt too ill to tolerate sex at all, although she was willing to make love to him and bring him to orgasm manually whenever he felt the need. But she wanted no such experience for herself, and he became very worried about this, though he didn't tell her. He was afraid, he told the therapist, that it meant "she didn't want" him anymore. And he missed very much the pleasure of giving her pleasure; he didn't want sex just for himself.

When their child was born Ray was excluded from the maternity ward by the rather old-fashioned hospital staff, and when the doctor came to tell him his child had been born, he asked only about Jan and went straight in to see her, "forgetting even to ask what it was." Jan told him they had a son, and they agreed that he was to be called Paul because Ray's mother had been named Pauline.

Jan settled easily and happily into motherhood, breast-feeding successfully from the start, and she formed a close and happy bond with the baby right away. But, well trained in psychology as she was, she was aware of the importance of including Ray in all dealings with the baby, and did her best to involve him. However, he was unwilling to change diapers. "They made me feel sick," he said, and he was equally unwilling to bathe the baby: "I thought I might hurt him."

Their sex life reestablished itself quickly, well before Jan's postnatal check-up, and she seemed to have lost none of her original drive. This was a great relief to

Ray, who had feared the loss of interest during pregnancy days had been a personal rejection. Her new eagerness now comforted him a good deal.

However, he now began to lose some of his own drive, and on three occasions could not complete intercourse because he lost his erection. Jan tried to reassure him that this was not important, a temporary effect, but he was so distressed that he wept.

In the resulting state of release he was able to tell Jan why he thought he was having the problem. Breast play had always been a very vital part of their love-making, partly because he knew Jan found it very arousing and partly because he enjoyed it for himself. "Playing with her breasts always made me feel so peaceful and right. It seemed more important than intercourse sometimes – just having intercourse without it wasn't the same." But, displaying the same sort of squeamishness he had about the baby's diapers, he felt he couldn't enjoy this with lactating breasts. They had changed, anyway, he said. "All big and hard, not the comfortable, beautifully soft cushions they had always been."

Jan did all she could to comfort him and tried to help him accept the changes in her body, but he felt he could not. Anyway, he told her, it bothered him that she couldn't enjoy this special lovemaking any more. She told him that it didn't matter, because feeding the baby gave her a lot of pleasure and satisfaction and helped her "to be ready for making love."

This had made him more depressed than ever, and he was unable to achieve an erection at all for some weeks; now the situation was reversed. Jan's sexual need was high, and she often came to bed after feeding the baby and settling him to sleep to try to arouse Ray; failing, she would persuade him to pet her to orgasm. "But I hated it," Ray said to the therapist. "It wasn't the way married love ought to be."

Jan decided to wean the baby earlier than she had intended, and, by the time he was three months old, he was on the bottle. Jan became a little depressed, and this flattened her sexual drive. For about two months the couple "drifted – we didn't seem to be as close as we had been. It was miserable."

They went to their family doctor, who put them both on antidepressant drugs for three months. Within another two months they had begun to reestablish their pattern of sexual activity. "By the time Paul was a year old we were all right again, but it had been a bad year. A very bad year," Raymond said.

Over the next two years Paul developed well and was an equable child, if a little timid in his dealings with other children. His father began to spend more time with him, and by the time he was three and fully toilet trained Ray was a willing helper. He would cheerfully take Paul to the toilet when the family was away from home, "which wasn't like me really – I'd been nearly sick at the thought of changing his diapers and couldn't stay in the room when Jan was doing it, but now I didn't mind."

Jan decided to go back to college in the evenings to get another degree. Ray first demurred, but after a lot of discussion he faced up to the fact that he was afraid of Jan becoming more "intellectual" than he was. With Jan's constant reassurance that she would remain as loving and as close to him as she had always been, he was able to accept what her studying involved – which was more time with Paul.

To both his own and Jan's surprise he took well to this. He bathed the little boy every night and put him to bed while his mother was at college, and he also chose to get up first in the mornings to get him out of bed and dress him. Jan was very happy and so was

Ray. He had to admit that he'd resented Paul's demands on Jan's time at first, but this was no longer true.

All went well, with Jan getting her degree and taking on some well-paid, part-time lecturing, and Paul started school successfully. Then Jan had an attack of summer diarrhea and vomiting while they were away on vacation, and as a result her contraceptive – the Pill – failed. Women are warned to use additional protection if they vomit, since they may have lost the Pill that way, but Jan forgot.

Ray was very upset at the news that Jan was pregnant again. He had been happy to settle for one child, he said. This was a bad world to rear big families in, and anyway, they were settled. They didn't need another child. But Jan could not contemplate an abortion, so the pregnancy was allowed to continue. Both of them were anxious throughout, both because of Jan's age (she was now thirty-four) because they had heard reports of older mothers giving birth to handicapped babies (an unjustified fear in fact), and also because she had, not realizing she was pregnant, continued to take the Pill for some time in the early days. This too has been said to cause damaged babies.

However, when the baby, a boy they named Edward, was born, he was a healthy and vigorous infant, and the birth was uncomplicated. But both parents remembered painfully the unhappy time that had followed Paul's birth, and they were somewhat apprehensive.

Jan offered not to breast-feed Edward. She knew that Ray had had difficulty coping with this the last time, and she thought he might again. However, Ray was well aware of her views on the value of breast-feeding and would not allow her to "make such a sacrifice." He told the therapist, "I'd learned a bit by now, what with Jan studying psychology, and I thought, it's just primitive jealousy. I can cope with it."

And cope he did, much to his own and Jan's relief. She breast-fed Edward and again felt a high sexual drive throughout, and Ray showed no obvious anxiety about it. He spent a lot of time with Paul to help him not to be jealous of his new brother (though in fact, as a now much more outgoing five-year-old, Paul was interested in the baby and seemed unperturbed by his arrival) and to keep Jan from being overloaded with work. Ray's sex drive did seem to diminish somewhat, and he had a few more episodes of losing his erection, but the couple talked it over in their usual sensible fashion and agreed that this was probably due not so much to an actual falling-off in his drive as to the marked increase in Jan's. "It really wasn't my fault – and Jan said so, too. Any man'd get tired because, bless her, she was really very turned-on there for a while."

Then the incident that triggered his breakdown occurred. It was a Sunday morning, and Ray got up to bring baby Edward from his crib – he was now six months old – to Jan in bed. He then went to the kitchen to make some coffee. Paul had meanwhile awakened and gone into his parents' room, where he climbed into bed next to his mother.

Jan explained to the therapist what had actually happened. "Paul watched me feeding the baby, as he often did, and started asking questions – he'd often asked them before – about where the milk came from, and how it got out of me, and how much there was, and then he said – and he'd never said this before – 'what does it taste like?' I told him I didn't know – sweet and milky, I imagined. Anyway, the baby liked it just as much as *he* had when he was tiny. Then he asked me again to tell him what was in it, and I tried to explain about the way my food changed inside me, thinking, I suppose, that this was a useful way to teach him some simple biology. Then he said again, 'What does it taste

like? Can I taste it?' And he looked up at me with a sort
of guarded expression. I thought – he's trying me out.
He's saying, does she love the baby more than me? Will
she let me do what the baby does? Too much psychology, maybe – anyway, that's the way I thought,
and I decided right then that I had to be offhand about
this and reassure him. I said, 'Can't you remember?'
and he said, 'No. Can I taste it now to remind me?'
and I said, 'If you like.' I had the baby at the left breast
at the time, and the right one was exposed, of course,
and Paul was sitting there on my right, on Ray's side of
the bed. Paul leaned over and took my nipple in his
mouth, and that was when Ray came in."

This was a difficult time in the psychotherapy because Ray became very agitated but he did calm down
eventually and explained what had happened next. "I
came in with the tray and I saw them in my bed with
my wife, both of them at her, and I felt sick. It looked
disgusting, seeing a huge fat baby hanging on one
breast and that enormous child on the other, and I just
threw the tray across the room and grabbed Paul – by
his hair, I think – and pulled him away. He screamed,
of course, and so did Jan, because I suppose he'd
clamped his jaws on her as a reaction, and he'd bitten
her. I could see her breast was bleeding. Then the baby
started to shriek and I didn't know what to do . . . ."

In fact he had fainted, and Jan coped with the situation as best she could. She soothed both screaming
children, and, when Ray regained consciousness she
helped him to lie down on the bed. He had said he felt
sick then, and vomited, and they agreed that he must
have "picked up a bug." He spent twenty-four hours in
bed and then seemed better when he got up. All seemed
to go on as before. But then the depression started
again and became the "nervous breakdown" that had
brought him to therapy.

The dynamics of this situation are fairly clear: a boy deprived of his mother when young, and despised by a successful father for being less gifted than himself, chose to fall in love with a girl both older and more intelligent than he was, thus providing himself with the missing factors in his life. His close dependence on Jan was more like a child's love than a sexual partner's, and their lovemaking, with its breast emphasis, displayed this, too. It was almost inevitable that such a man would have difficulty accepting, without jealousy and resentment, another male's involvement in his relationship with his mother-wife, even a male who was his own infant son. And the mother's illness which had accompanied the pregnancy and his birth had added to the threat the child himself seemed to be making. That Jan breast-fed this interloper added to the stress, and when she also showed signs of being sexually aroused by caring for him, Ray reacted strongly by losing some of his own sexual drive – the classic response of the rejected or defeated male in any group of mammals. The same thing happens to male baboons and chimpanzees when they are supplanted by younger rivals.

Jan's own insights had helped them to weather that difficult period, and Ray had coped better still when Paul reached an age when he no longer needed his mother's intimate care to the same degree; it was significant, the therapist felt, that Ray and Paul had achieved a better relationship once Ray took over the bathing, washing and dressing routines. He had, in effect, supplanted his rival and could therefore relax and allow himself to enjoy the child's company.

Had the second baby been a girl, then Ray might have been able to take it more easily, but the combination of the new baby's gender – another rival – and the unexpected sight when he had returned to his bedroom – his own territory – had totally fragmented all his attempts to deny his anxiety and his resentment. Hence the breakdown.

Therapy was in fact successful; Ray had learned from Jan over the years and was an intelligent and willing patient. He is now well, and the family is happy. The boys are now aged eight and three. Ray and Jan are saving up to send the boys to boarding school. Jan feels it is the better form of education for them, and she also suspects that their puberty could be a difficult time for Ray. It would be better if a certain amount of space were created around them. Also, she would like to enroll in further study and extend her academic life, and this would be more difficult with boisterous pre-adolescents to deal with all the time.

Not all fathers of sons display quite such dramatic responses to their deeper feelings, but paternal jealousy of a new baby is undoubtedly common. Virtually every popular baby book ever written in English has included earnest advice to a new mother "not to neglect" her husband because of the baby. Some of them also make the point that a father may show more resentment of a baby boy than of a girl, though only a few show this insight.

It is interesting that in this family plans are already in hand to send away Ray's "rivals," the two boys, when they approach puberty. Whether the tradition of sending young males away from the risk of the wrath of the older one developed from this – and it is an ancient tradition; in medieval Europe, rich men's sons were sent to other rich men's castles as pages at this age, and boarding schools have existed for centuries – or whether it developed because the older males were not willing to tolerate the young ones on their patch of ground, it is hard to say. But the tradition is there, and it is interesting to say the least that in these days of what is occasionally sentimental adulation of family life it lingers on. The relationship between a man and his sons can be fraught with problems, and separation may be their best resolution.

8
Mothers and Daughters

"WE WILL HAVE A FAMILY, a boy for you, a girl for me . . ." The hit song of the hit musical of 1925, *No, No, Nanette* said it so well for so many people that it's been a standard song ever since. The idea that lies behind it is that if a man welcomes a son as the ultimate in self perpetuation, women welcome a daughter in the same way. And it may well be true, but for rather different reasons.

For a start, a woman feels no guilt about the inequality of the reproductive burden – quite the reverse, in fact. It is not uncommon for a newly delivered mother, in whose memory the discomforts of giving birth are still very green, to feel and express loud resentment. As a pupil midwife at Guy's Hospital in London, which included many outspoken wives of longshoremen among its patients, I became used to hearing new mothers share jokes that, like all the best jokes, revealed important feelings.

"I'll tie a knot in it when I get home to him – this'll be the last time *I'm* in here"; "It's going to cost him dear this time – new coat and a bag, that's what he's getting me to say thank you with. Not that he knows it yet . . ."; "I'm going to get me a cat – he can try and see what satisfaction he gets out of kittens"; there were several more which were very pungent and much more expressive but are also unfortunately unprintable.

So a daughter isn't welcomed as any sort of sop to guilt in the way that fathers welcome sons as I described in the previous chapter, though perhaps a woman who has found her labor particularly distressing might feel guilt toward her female baby. How cruel to have produced another female to suffer as she has!

Nor is a daughter welcomed as a source of financial or dynastic satisfaction. In no way will this baby girl bring fortune into a family that is part of a patriarchal society. She is more likely to be seen as a financial liability. Girls are regarded as more expensive than boys in many ways – even though, in fact, most traditionally minded families spend more on rearing a son (say, by paying tuition for costly private education) than they do on a daughter. Perhaps the idea that girls are expensive comes from the all-too-common belief that women are genetically extravagant, actually born more concerned with spending money on personal fripperies than with being serious about earning it.

If it is considered possible that the girl will grow up to become a woman who does manage to make money by being successful, this would not be regarded as likely to benefit her own family, for she will marry, take another man's name, and in exchange she will give him the benefit of her abilities. And there is every reason for people to feel like this. How often do you see newspaper reports of a successful woman in which she is described as a particular man's wife, rather than as another's daughter? Far more often than you see a man described as someone's husband, that's for sure – though his father, if he is illustrious enough, may well be mentioned.

Then what about the sense of alliance? This is indeed powerful. Right from the beginning daughters are often regarded by their mothers as helpers, comforters, sharers of feminine pleasure – "little girls are much more fun to buy clothes for" – and above all as *reliable*. "A son is a son till he gets him a wife – a daughter's a daughter the whole of her life" is one of the oldest of English proverbs, and it is still quoted and believed.

The extraordinary thing about this saying and its variants is that it does in fact run directly counter to the ideas that lie behind the dynastic tradition. These suggest that a son at marriage brings his wife and her fortune into the family while a daughter takes it out; yet the proverb implies the direct opposite! We are indeed a very ambivalent bunch.

And having mentioned ambivalence let's get back to the notion of a woman wanting a daughter during pregnancy in the same way that a man wants a son. In fact, it seems that in a great many cases she doesn't. Women, too, seem to feel that the production of a son is special in a way that the production of a daughter is not. The woman who is the mother of a brood of daughters tends to be regarded as a dominant, "hen pecking" type, and certainly her husband will receive sympathy from other men (and some women!) for having to live his life with a pack of females. The mother of a brood of sons, on the other hand, is seen as a very admirable figure, surrounded by a group of splendid fellows, and certainly she is unlikely to receive any commiseration for not having a member of her own sex in the household. Even intelligent, liberal-minded women may subscribe to this attitude.

"I look at my best friend sometimes who has three daughters, and I think of my two boys as well as my daughter, and I feel smug, as though I'm better than her because she couldn't quite manage it. Which is nonsense, of course. I mean, I know perfectly well that the children's sex has nothing to do with me – that it was my husband's sperm which decided that issue. But I can't help it – when I look at Ann, I think – poor old Ann. When my second baby was born and was a girl I wasn't disappointed, exactly, but it took me six months to realize I had a daughter, and to get at all used to the idea. I'd always seen myself as having a dozen boys, you see. Never as having daughters. Yet I enjoy women's company, and I'm on reasonable enough terms with my own mother – it's odd, isn't it? And now, of course, I love my daughter dearly – and we're real allies. There are times when I get a lovely sense of rapport – she understands me in a way my boys never do. She's supportive, helpful – lovely to have around. The boys are often thoughtless, wilful, unconcerned about my feelings – or anyone else's, come to that – altogether more selfish. Yet I still think – poor old Ann. Which as an educated woman, with strong political feelings, makes me feel positively ashamed sometimes."

She needn't feel too ashamed. Hers is an attitude shared by many, and it is only in very recent years that it has even been suggested that such an attitude was in any way "wrong." When Jane Austen's *Pride and Prejudice* was first published, its delighted readers enjoyed enormously the subtle satire about Mrs. Bennett's efforts to get her too-numerous daughters suitably married – but never for a moment did they question the underlying assumption that having a number of daughters for whom husbands must be found is a major family disaster. And many of the people who read it for the first time today, well over 150 years after it was written, will find the same pleasure and make the same acceptance.

We have already seen that male reaction to male offspring can be closely linked with sexual jealousy.

Does this happen to the mothers of daughters in the same way?

Of course it does, but it may be much harder to recognize, for a reason that is so glaringly obvious it is almost inevitably overlooked.

A mother gives a baby all its intimate care, whatever its gender. Her physical contact with her infant is regarded by herself and by everyone around her as inevitable and normal, which is why a man's sexual jealousy of his son may seem to a mother to be particularly incomprehensible. "How can a man possibly see his baby as a sexual threat?" she will reason. "It's nonsense, rubbish made up by these psychology people." Yet if her husband, her man, the one she has chosen to love and share sexuality with, were to spend as much time in intimate physical contact with their infant daughter as she does with an infant son, I suspect she would begin to understand. If part of the parents' love-making which is so special to them were to be shared by him with their baby daughter in the way she shares it with a baby son when she breast-feeds him, would she be so lacking in sympathy? Surely she would not. But it can be a painful lesson to learn.

> I am a new mother. I sit in the theater beside my husband, staring down at the stage over my shelf of a bust; no longer can this conglomerate of flesh, tightly straining in its binder and feeling so full that I think I will burst, be called breasts. They are melded together into a "Bust" that looks and feels as though I have been upholstered. I say the words beneath my breath. I am a Mother. And my husband looks at me inquiringly and I shake my head and smile into the half-darkness. We are close, we have a relationship that we have worked at for three years and which shines in our lives like the

glow of a fire that we are sure will never go out, yet I cannot share this with him. I am a Mother. He is not.

I think of the infant who lies in the hospital nursery, where they have offered to look after her while we celebrate my birthday. I have a daughter, and I mouth the word inside my head. I have a daughter. It means little, for I had meant to be able to say, I have a son. Like so many other mothers-to-be it had been a boy I had wanted to produce. I had always said that the reason I wanted a boy is that I have for many years not been able to think of my own mother except with pain and fear and the hatred that covers so many other complex feelings. I had said I could not build a relationship with a female, because the one that had been my model had been so disastrous. Yet I had done it. I had produced a daughter, and far from feeling disappointed or distanced from this girl child, I know her to be mine in a way a boy could not have been. We belong together, I tell myself in the dark theater, as no child and mother ever belonged together, and the tears of pleasure drip off my nose and I sniff and feel foolish. Postpartum depression, the doctors call it. Baby blues the other women call it. But I know it's because I am a mother of a daughter that I weep.

In two days we take the baby home. She lies in her crib in the bedroom that belongs to us and I am uneasy. I do not like to see her crib there, and in the wisdom of my nursing training I tell my husband it is unhealthy for a baby to sleep in its parents' room. She must be taken out at night, I say. She can be in here in the daytime but at night she must sleep in the living room of our tiny apartment. Healthier for her, I insist. Better for us, too, I say, and inside I think without words – this is my place, my place where I live with my man. She shall not be here.

We are happy together, my daughter and I. I bathe her and dress her and hold her and listen to her. I change her diapers and one day, she wriggles around in such a way that she lies on my lap with her head against my belly and her legs parallel with mine and I look down on the smooth skin of her belly, at the upturned smiling lines that are her groin and the little slit of her genitals and suddenly I am a small child again looking down at my own body and thinking how nice my smiling lines look.

There is another moment of such rapport when one day I bathe her. I do as I always have – I soap my hand rather than a harsh washcloth and rub the soap over her body and she enjoys it; or seems to, lying smiling in the water. And then I soap my hand again, and wash her bottom and her legs and slip my hand between them to wash her vulva and for a moment she stops smiling and the memory is so sharp I wince. I feel the harshness of soap on my own vulva as my mother washes me in a basin, standing on a table. "It stings! It hurts!" I shriek at her but she laughs and says, "Rubbish! Of course it doesn't! Open up – you must be washed, dirty girl." At once I take my soapy hand away from my daughter's vulva and splash water, gently and kindly. Oh, I am a good mother. I understand what it is to be a little girl. I have rapport.

And then one evening when she is in her crib and I am in our little kitchen cooking dinner for my husband and for me, he comes home early, and I quickly turn down the heat on the stove and put down the spoon I am holding and dry my hands and go to greet him at the door. But I am too late. He is in the apartment, he has closed the front door and has gone straight to our bedroom. He is beside the crib and has bent down and picked her up, and is holding her close and crooning to her, standing there in his overcoat and still cold from the outside air. He looks at me for a brief moment and smiles and says, "How is she?" and looks down at her again, and she lies in his arms and looks up at him and smiles and he smiles back. I am outside, I am rejected, I am alone. How is *she*? How dare he ask? How dare she be there in my bedroom, taking precedence over me? I hate him, I hate her, I hate myself. I am so filled with hate I cannot think.

That night I cry, and he is tender and makes me talk, and I tell him, and am grateful. It will be all right now, I have verbalized it, I have taken out that stupid sick feeling and seen it for what it is. I am jealous. I *was* jealous. Now we have talked about it we can be close again, my daughter and I. The jealousy is gone. Until the next time.

To an extent, of course, a woman's reaction to her daughter's femininity will be a reflection of her view of herself. Does she see a woman's role as being deferential and gentle and weak? If she does she will expect her daughter to behave in this way from her infancy upward, as though these behavior patterns were born with her like her eye color or the shape of her ears. And because she believes her to be so, she may well find that the little girl does, in fact, respond in just that sort of way – or at least will *appear* to do so. That is, the mother's interpretation of her baby's behavior will be based on her view of what it ought to be.

When the baby cries her mother will see this not as a

noisy demand for attention, but as an expression of distress and a cry for help. When she is fretful and shows signs of being unwilling to be put in her crib to sleep, her mother will see her behavior as meaning she is lonely and needs reassurance and loving.

But if a mother has been made to feel by her own upbringing that females are shrill naggers and whiners, that they are tiresome, troublesome things, then she will interpret her daughter's behavior in those terms.

And if she has been filled with anger by the way she has all her life been pushed out of the sun, as she sees it, because of her gender, she will interpret her daughter's crying and demands for attention as expressions of the same feelings of resentment and rage.

The most important thing about such reactions is that they can become self-fulfilling prophecies. The mother who sees her child's cries as expressions of distress made by a weak and tender creature in an extreme of need will respond with comfort and care as soon as she hears the first whimper and will go on doing so as her child grows older. The result will be that she will to an extent train her to be extra dependent and clinging. This is the sort of mother who holds a small girl back when she wants to explore and encourages her in all behavior that is clinging and fearful – but allows a boy greater latitude.

The mother who regards crying as a sign of whining, nagging behavior, on the other hand, will probably refuse to respond and will leave the child to cry for a long time before going to satisfy her needs – and then will do so in a scolding grudging way. And once again she will train the child to be the demanding nag she already thinks she is, having been born that way.

The angry mother, however, is unlikely to make her child as angry as she is. It is the "all-females-are-naggers" mother who produces that sort of emotion in her child. In fact it is possible that a woman who admires her baby's cries as an expression of justifiable rage will go to her child when she makes them, to express her approval in physical handling and loving. And that is most likely to train a child to cry less, rather than more loudly. Yet another double bind for the woman struggling to be free?

Far-fetched theorizing? Up to a point, of course, much of the foregoing will seem so, for I have dealt in broad general reactions, quite unmodified by individual personality differences, lifestyles and cultures. But all I have seen of mothers handling their babies – and that has been a great deal over the years – confirms me in the belief that allowing for differences in education, attitudes and personality, all mothers *do* respond differently to their babies according to their gender; that these responses are broadly the same when it comes to the way a boy is handled (because women have never been boys and lack any real sense of rapport with them, finding them to an extent alien creatures) but vary when handling a girl according to the way the mother sees herself.

So it is that from the very start a woman molds her daughter's thinking, behavior and view of herself in a way that is extremely effective; she is very likely indeed to make that girl either a true mirror image of herself, or else a reversed one – but either way it will be an accurate representation of the mother.

I know that, in my own life, I have over and over again found myself doing things, saying things, behaving in a way that, had I managed to apply objective intellectual thought, I would have rejected. But because it was an emotional imperative with me to do or say the precise opposite of everything I thought my mother would have done in every circumstance, I was not really in full control of myself. *She* was, just as she had been in my infancy. I am still working at finding my escape.

Of course, in most traditional families, the mother is not the only influence as the girl grows. Fathers, and their views of femininity and masculinity, also have a considerable effect.

9
Fathers and Daughters

"THANK HEAVEN FOR little girls, for little girls grow sweeter every day" is very explicit indeed about the sexual attraction of prepubertal females. The eroticism is not even lightly disguised: "Those little eyes, so helpless and appealing, one day will flash and send you crashing through the ceiling."

It is an interesting fact that in nearly all Western countries small girls are seen as potentially sexual creatures in a way that small boys are not. In popular iconography – greeting cards, calendars, decorated boxes of chocolate and advertisements – boys are shown as mischievous imps, dirty, noisy, greedy and more likely to be emotionally involved with a dog than a person. Little girls, on the other hand, are depicted as soft, sweet and yielding, very sociable and charming, and are shown wearing scaled-down copies of the clothes grown women used to wear – seductive frills and tight waists to accentuate a feminine shape the children do not yet have.

And it is not only in such fantasy images that little girls are glossed with eroticism; every beach and swimming pool is littered with small girls, aged well under ten, wearing bikini swimsuits complete with a breast-covering over their undeveloped nipples. None of the little boys are ever put into junior versions of jockstraps, however.

It is inevitable that fathers share some of the same feelings about small girls as other men and project those feelings on to their own small daughters. They are encouraged to do so by the attitudes of women. They, too, seem to see the young female child as sexual in a way they do not regard the boy. A woman taking three or four children of both sexes aged under ten out for the day has no problems when the children want to use a toilet. She will take both boys and girls to a public women's toilet and none of the other women there will turn a hair. But when a man is out with those same children and they want to pee, the chances are that he will not take the little girl into the men's toilet; he would rather accost a total stranger outside the women's loo and ask her to look after the little girl's needs.

Is this because most public men's toilets provide open urinals for the users, and there is the Awful Risk of a small girl seeing an exposed adult penis if she enters those hallowed walls? Hardly; small boys are commonly taken into toilet cubicles by women, and no one feels there is any dreadful risk if a male child observes a woman pull down her pants. It seems to me very likely that small boys are regarded as sexually unaware while girls most certainly are not. Even the way we actually dress children (rather than merely depict them in drawings on greeting cards) displays this. Small girls' clothes are much more likely to mimic adult secondary sexual characteristics such as tight-waisted, full-hipped dresses, short enough to display bottoms rounded out by being encased in more frills. Boys' suits are not enlarged at the shoulders to imitate male broadness, nor are their crotches padded to simulate developed genitalia.

The fact that men see small girls as sexually interesting does not display any "evil" in them; far from it.

Adults of both genders certainly recognize and respond to the sexuality of their opposite-sex young, but women, it seems, are more able to suppress this response in themselves. It is somehow less acceptable for a woman to admire the potential for sexual pleasure that is hidden in a small boy's shape than for men to do the same with little girls. Is this because women, in their maternal role, are so intimately involved with the direct physical care of small children that they need a built-in block to protect them – and the children – from being aroused by such contact? It's impossible to say: all we can be certain of is that men have tacit social permission to respond to the sexuality of little girls.

But side by side with this permission there is public anxiety. Small girls are regarded as under almost constant threat of sexual attack by "bad" men – i.e., men who have taken a step too far along the road in recognizing young sexuality. It is little girls who are warned not to talk to strangers; little girls who are not allowed to go out and about on their own; little girls who are threatened with the risks of taking sweets or car rides from men – *even men they know.*

All this can create considerable problems for fathers, for families and, of course, for children.

Alex and Helen had been married seven years before they decided they could no longer live together in any sort of amity. They planned a "civilized" divorce that would not hurt the children, six-year-old Donald and five-year-old Donna. Alex moved out of the family house in the suburbs to an apartment in the middle of town, and Helen took a job as a dental assistant – she had been well trained and could earn a considerable amount of money – and employed a live-in maid to take care of the children while she was at work. It was agreed that Alex would have access to the children freely but without any formal structure. He didn't want his relationship with them to deteriorate into a series of "Dad's Sundays" as had happened to some of his divorced friends.

Helen had little time or energy for a social life of her own, but Alex on the other hand seemed to blossom once the couple split up. He was a dentist (they had met over his dental chair), so Helen heard all the time from mutual friends and contacts what he was doing. He had a lot of girl friends and generally lived it up. And although Helen assured her friends that she didn't mind, that she had lost sexual interest in Alex long before they actually broke up, she was, her friends agreed, rather irritated by it all. And they went on telling her all that was going on, in the way that the friends of divorced people so often seem to enjoy doing.

One Friday afternoon Helen passed out at work. She had been suffering from a heavy cold caught from the children, and though they were now back at school, she had slept poorly during the time they were both ill. There was nothing sinister about her collapse, but her employer, a rather fussy old man, panicked and had her sent to the hospital as an emergency.

When Helen regained consciousness and was able to think clearly she panicked in her turn; Friday was her maid's half day, and she had the afternoon off. Normally Helen herself picked the children up from school on Fridays, and now here she was in a hospital miles away. She couldn't possibly get there in time.

She tried to telephone the school to ask if one of the teachers could look after the children until someone could come for them, but the school phone was out of order. She then telephoned Alex, almost hysterical with anxiety and still very shaken by her own collapse, and asked him to pick up the children. He assured her he would, but as he was in the middle of a difficult case, he asked his junior partner Joe if he would go instead. Which he did.

Joe arrived at the school about twenty minutes after the children had been let out, and most of them had disappeared. Only Donald and Donna stood at the school gates, looking mournful.

Joe knew the childrens' appearance from the photograph Alex kept on his desk, and greeted them, told them that their Dad had sent him to pick them up and take them to his office. Donald at once agreed cheerfully to get into the car, but Donna flatly refused. She stood holding on to the school fence and just shook her head vigorously when the young man tried to persuade her to get into the car.

Inexperienced with children, he lost his patience and tried to grab her, and she turned and wriggled through an opening in the fence and ran back up the path. It was impossible for the young man to follow her, and when he asked Donald, sitting happily in the car, to go after his sister, he wouldn't.

"She's soppy. Take no notice of her."

"Where do you suppose she's gone?" the young man asked.

The little boy shrugged. "To her friend's, I suppose," he said indifferently. "There's a back way out she can go through to get to her house. Does this switch make the roof go up and down? Can I try it?"

The young man, now thoroughly irritated and very aware of the fact that one of his own patients was due shortly, decided to drive around to the back of the school to see if he could find Donna. After much hunting through the suburban roads, however, he admitted defeat and took Donald to his father, explaining what had happened.

By this time Helen had been discharged from the

hospital and had arrived at Alex's office to pick up the children and take them home. When Joe arrived without Donna she became hysterical, Alex lost his temper, and a noisy argument followed during which Donald became alarmed and screamed loudly.

The police were called to help find the missing child, and they checked at both the friend's house and the family house, but she seemed to have disappeared. Helen was taken home under sedation by a friend of hers, and Alex set out to search for Donna on his own.

At 11 P.M. she arrived at his apartment in town, exhausted and very distressed. She had, it appeared, *walked* all the way from her school in the suburbs to the apartment, losing her way on many occasions, and going around in circles. It was incredible that she had found the place at all, only knowing the route from having made it several times in Alex's car. But somehow she had.

Alex at once phoned the police and then Helen. She was asleep, and the friend had gone home, since the living-in maid had returned. Alex wanted to protect Helen from any more disturbance after such an anxious day, so he told the maid not to wake her up from her sedated sleep, but to tell her first thing in the morning that Donna was safe with her father. He then put Donna to bed in his own bed and went to sleep himself.

The following morning was Saturday, and he had no patients, he slept late, and the exhausted child also slept on. At 9:30 A.M. Helen arrived, white with rage and still almost hysterical with anxiety. Her maid, it seemed, had told her some garbled story about last night's phone call, and Helen hadn't waited to get it clear; she had just driven full speed to Alex's apartment where she was let in by his maid when she rang the bell.

She walked straight into Alex's bedroom when the

maid said that as far as she knew he was still asleep, and when she saw Donna asleep beside her father she flew at Alex and began to hit him. It took a long time to calm her down, and Alex, himself enraged by this attack, hit her back, an action observed by the enthralled maid.

The following week Helen instituted proceedings in court, asking for Alex to be prevented from having contact with the children on his own. She asked the court to say he could only see the children when she herself was present. Her reason was that he was unfit to be trusted with a small girl. He had sent a strange man to collect her from school when he knew perfectly well the child had been warned all her life about the danger of ever accepting rides with strangers, and then he had shared his bed with her. On both these grounds, she said, he had clearly proven that he could not be trusted with a little girl. At no point in her complaint did she mention his treatment of Donald.

The court agreed to her request without asking for much other evidence, and Alex now sees his children only rarely; the court decreed a weekly visit, but it is often "inconvenient" for Helen to arrange the day Alex wants, and anyway, the whole business of the visits is so unpleasant, with Helen watching every move he makes toward Donna, that they are no pleasure for anyone.

Alex says that in another few years, whether he likes it or not, his relationship with the children will have ended. He also thinks that Helen reacted as she did out of a mixture of resentment of his active sex life since their divorce, seeing it as evidence of an unbridled sexuality in him (their marriage had foundered because Helen had said he was oversexed, while he found her "frigid"), and jealousy of his love for his daughter. He regards Helen's teachings about the dreadful risks strange men pose to little girls as an expression of her anti-sex feeling, and is very angry at the way he's been labeled as a "dirty old man" of a father. Helen on her part denies vehemently that she is imputing anything evil to Alex that isn't obvious for all to see.

Obviously in any individual set of relationships there will be complex strands of feeling and behavior that modify the effects of basic drives. But it seems fairly clear that, in this case, the idea that a man could pose a sexual threat to his own daughter was easily accepted – not just by Helen, but by the court to which she appealed.

If these social attitudes cause problems for men as fathers to daughters when there is a wife around – albeit an estranged one – what about the dilemma of the single-parent family made up of a father and his daughter(s)? Their problems can be even greater.

No one will pretend that being a single-parent family is ever easy. Mothers alone (and there are more of them than there are fathers because of society's tendency, expressed through its divorce courts, to assume that a child is always better off in its mother's care) have many anxieties. In Britain the majority of such families are below the poverty line, receiving money from the state and still barely making ends meet. But single mothers are more likely to meet with sympathy from the powers-that-be in their attempts to keep a family together than are single fathers.

Before my wife died last year I made her one promise, and I'll move heaven and earth to keep it. I told her that I'd look after Mary, who is now ten, and Susan, who is now eleven.

We'd been a lovely happy family, not rich, you know, but managing all right, and when Lily got cancer I thought the end of the world had come. And it had, really, because after she was dead I wanted to die, too. We'd been together since we were kids – we'd been in the same class at school, and right from the time we were twelve or so, we sort of went together. And when she died it was hell. But I'd promised about the girls and they needed me so I had to soldier on, didn't I?

It wasn't so bad the first few months. There was a bit of insurance money to help, and the people at the factory where I've worked for fifteen years – I'm a toolbench operator there – did all they could, letting me go early to pick the girls up from school and everything. And the neighbors were very good. But they forget after a bit, don't they? Life goes on, you see, and once the memory of it all goes, well, you can't blame people for sort of losing interest. So the neighbors weren't as available as they had been, and when Mary had a deal of illness – she ended up having her tonsils out, but for a few months there she was in bed at home more often than she was at school, poor little lass – and my supervisor at the factory got a bit stroppy, said I had to keep better hours or I'd be out – after all those years, too – I was in real trouble.

Anyway, early this year I went down to the welfare office. Told them it was getting difficult and said what I needed was someone to come and be there when the girls got out of school, to see they got their teas and watch over them till I got home from the factory at 6:30 P.M. Only a couple of hours, really. I didn't want any housework done, or anything – I do it myself, go down to the laundromat every Saturday afternoon, iron on Sunday morning while dinner's cooking, dust and sweep on Sunday afternoon – but I just couldn't lose any more time in the week. And though the girls were all right to come home safe on their own from school, I wouldn't have them alone for that two hours. It's not the best neighborhood in the world, where we live, and anyway, they aren't used to it. Their Mum was always there when they were little, and they're still entitled to a happy home. I don't want them to turn into any of these latch-key kids. Anyway, like I said, I asked the welfare people. And the first thing they said was, 'We'll take them into care.' I ask you! Over my dead body, I told them, we stick together, me and my girls, and no one's going to split us up till the day some fella comes along and marries 'em, and that's all there is to it, and couldn't they just let me have someone to help in the afternoons, two hours a day, Monday to Friday?

'Couldn't afford that,' they said, 'costs money,' they said, and I had to laugh. I mean, how much would it cost them to keep my girls in one of their damned hostels or orphanages or whatever? A bloody sight more!

Then I said to them, why is it when Mrs. Cooper who's got three kids about the same age as mine, lives three doors away, how is it when her old man took off with a woman he'd picked up at the local pub and just dumped her, no money, nothing, they didn't take her kids away? She gets someone to help from the welfare, more money'n what I get from working forty-eight hours a week in a factory, and all you can do to me, whose wife was as good a woman as ever breathed, is try to take my kids away from me. If that's what I pay my taxes for I honestly wonder – what sort of country is it?

Anyway, I managed. I got this retired lady from up the road, nice old gal she is and the girls like her, and she comes in and I pay her. It isn't easy, and I've had to cut down a lot on the food we buy, but its worth it. I mean, I'd rather we lived on scraps together than have the girls living on steak and ice cream in some sort of orphanage.

But that's not all. Like I said, I'd been down to the welfare office, and once they know about you, my God, but they watch! There's this nosy old social worker keeps coming around – 'Just stopped by,' she says, 'to see how you're getting by,' she says, but she's not fooling me. She's looking for trouble, an excuse to take the girls away from me. She started talking the other day about how I was going to help them over their personal lives – said it as though it was something disgusting! Did I want her to tell them about their periods and such, and I told her, I don't need any such help, and neither do they. Their Mum and me, we understood each other and we understood our girls. They knew a lot even before she died, young as they were. Lily knew she hadn't got long, you see, and she told them some things early, and anyway I don't have any shame about it. I can tell them what they need to know, and help them get what they need for their periods and that sort of thing, though of course it won't be for a while. And she made me feel really awful the way she looked at me, that woman, as though I was some sort of dirty old man. Yet there's Mrs. Cooper with her two boys as well as her girl, and no one ever thinks she's not fit to rear her boys just because she's a woman. So why should they think I can't rear my girls just because I'm their Dad?

She's still coming around, that damned social worker, and I don't dare let on what I really feel, because you never known – if I got her upset she might make a fuss and go to the courts and get my girls taken from me no matter how hard I fight. And I promised Lily.

So far we have looked at the relationships separated by a generation – parents and children. But what about another type of family relationship that is extremely close, that can be profoundly affected by emotions quite as intense as those of parent-child links, and which can have a lifelong effect on its participants – brothers and sisters?

10
Brothers and Sisters

THERE IS SOMETHING particularly warming about the concept of brotherhood. The word denotes a closeness, a mutually supporting group of people who are tied by love rather than mere duty, but who at the same time acknowledge that the tie demands unswerving loyalty. It is a nonjudgmental word in that it can be applied to any sort of group of men. There can be a brotherhood of holy men such as monks (the word friar derives from the French for brother, *frère*) or of lay members of a church, or a brotherhood of thieves and rascals.

Sisterhood is a less attractive word. It has a chilly sound to it, almost life-denying. A sisterhood, one feels, is made up of sex-hating virgins. There is no rollicking sound in "sisterhood" as there is in "brotherhood." In fact, the most well-known image conjured up by the word sisterhood is probably that of the three witches in *Macbeth*.

What relevance do these words have to the actual relationships from which they derive? How much are brothers part of a brotherhood? To what extent do sisters feel they belong to a sisterhood? And it is interesting that there is no matching word for a group of mixed-sex siblings.

The question is not merely a semantic one. Society is, after all, a family of families. Macrocosm and microcosm. And as society as a whole sees brotherhood and sisterhood, so, it is reasonable to assume, do brothers and sisters relate within a family.

It is possibly true that brothers often manage to build a close, mutually supportive and lifelong relationship, squabbling sometimes but offering a united face to the outside world – and indeed to other members of the immediate family – while sisters by and large do not. Their union may be close when they are young, but when puberty arrives, it is very likely to be split by the demands of their own sexuality. "Sisters, sisters – there were never such devoted sisters – Lord help the mister who comes between me and my sister, and Lord help the sister who comes between me and my man." – a funny song because it reflects what many sisters know about the quality of their relationship with these other women.

Such sweeping generalizations having been put up, they must immediately be shot down by particular examples that do not fit the mold. There are brothers who hate each other's guts (and where would romantic novelists be without plots in which Good Brother foils Bad Brother?), sisters who are so united that not even lovers and childbearing can put a hair between them, and all shades of relationships in between. For every band of brothers who form a cosa nostra, another plays out Cain and Abel rivalries over and over again.

But one thing is clear. However important the relationship that exists between a parent and a child, or between a pair of lovers, married or otherwise, the one that exists between children of the same parents is of great significance whether it is peaceful or warlike. So great in fact that most only children are pitied, not only by outsiders but by themselves as well. To be brother-and-sisterless is to be deprived.

The aspect of the sibling relationship about which the majority of parents are most concerned is jealousy.

Over and over again letters sent to advice columnists ask the same basic question.

> My little girl is now eighteen months old, and I am pregnant again. How can I prevent her from suffering from jealousy when the new baby comes?

Book after book on child care devote great swathes of print to offering the answer, which is absurd, because of course jealousy cannot be prevented. Nor should it be feared or regarded with disapproval, for it is an inevitable and indeed desirable emotion in a person who is aware of being loved. There would be something deeply wrong in the parent-child relationship if the child were not deeply alarmed and threatened by the sudden arrival of a rival.

Parents would find this easier to understand if they imagined a much-loved spouse coming home one day and saying, "You're a marvelous wife [husband]. In fact, you're so marvelous, and I love you so much, that I'm going to have another one just like you. But you mustn't be jealous."

So, in a child who is loved, the appearance of a new sibling must be seen as a source of pain – the fear of loss of the parents' love and acceptance. "Now they've got a new one, they won't want me."

Children need to learn how to handle these fears, how to allow the feelings they create to arise in them and then ebb away. But rarely are children given any help in doing this. They are taught instead to be afraid of their own fears, because when they express them their parents show anger, which may be interpreted by the children as signs of the very rejection they fear. So they feel more fear and again are punished for it, until at last they learn to suppress it. They have not rid themselves of it, nor stopped feeling it, yet their parents often think they have. "Oh no, no jealousy at all," they assure inquiring friends. "Tommy loves the new baby, don't you, dear? Gives her his toys and watches her all the time, hangs over the crib looking at her for ages."

All these actions are in fact clear evidence of the older child's fear and resentment. In "giving his toys" to the interloper he is trying to buy her off. "I'll give you these – now you get the hell out of here" is what is implied. The watching could be for signs of weakness, an almost animal-like vigilance against an enemy, but very often it is the child's dissimulation. He has found, perhaps by accident, the sort of behavior to show to his sibling which will please his mother. So he shows it. But he may well bestow a sharp pinch when the parental back is turned.

By the time the second child, in this case a younger sister, is old enough to feel the fear of loss of parental love and attention herself, the older child's suppressed jealousy may be so far below the surface that he doesn't even know he feels it any more. He will feel a closeness to his rival, born of propinquity. To earn the love of a child you have only to spend a lot of time with him or her. Once you and your smell and your sound, and possibly your taste, are imprinted firmly on the child's memory, the attachment will be formed. And it will last a long time, probably a lifetime. We may call it love, but basically it is mere habit, similar to the feeling that is called "love of country." The scenery in which you grow up is the scenery you know best, so you love it best.

The same applies to love of siblings. Later on, when intellect begins to move in and modify these early impressions, a deeper feeling of attachment may develop and be strong enough to deserve the label "love." But not always. Many brothers and sisters grow up attached, but never really loving each other in the way adults love their children or their sexual partners. And after all, why should children love their siblings? Adults choose their sex partners, choose to have offspring. This element of choice makes love much more possible. Brothers and sisters are forced on each other.

But, of course, some learn to love fiercely and protectively very early in life, and a very touching sight it can be when a small four-year-old carefully feeds a two-year-old, or a busy six-year-old steers a nervous five-year-old through the intricacies of the first day at school.

As in all family relationships, attachments between brothers and sisters are profoundly modified by many factors. The first is the individual personality. Some children are born with friendly, adaptable natures, while others seem to come into the world equipped with a suspicious disposition and a rigid approach to the pains of living.

Then there is the position in the family to take into account; oldest children have a different view of the world than middle or younger children. They may see themselves always as "put-upon," supplanted, rejected. Or they may see themselves as superior, the natural boss. Youngest children have a mythology all their own (the youngest son is always the hero in fairy stories, the one who gets the princess and her kingdom), but they may in fact feel themselves to be congenitally inferior. They may never be able to come to terms with the realization that, however hard they try and however much time passes, they can never catch up with the rest of the family – i.e., the world. On the other hand, they may be selfish, demanding and spoiled.

Much depends on parental, especially maternal, attitudes. A woman who enjoys babies more than she enjoys older children will give special status to the youngest and "spoil" that child, while one who feels the opposite will give special regard to her oldest and turn him or her into a superior bossy-boots.

Then, of course, gender rears its head. A son may receive very different treatment from a daughter, and as a result will regard his sister(s) in the light of his own status. When sons are admired and desired by parents but daughters are considered second-class family members, the brotherly attitude will be a lordly one, perhaps protective and dismissive, while the sister(s) may respond by pampering the younger boys and being deferential – if reluctantly – to older ones. The Victorian children's writer E. Nesbit showed clearly in her popular books, such as *The Phoenix and the Carpet* and *Five Children and It*, how such families operated. And Joyce Grenfell, a British actress and songwriter with a sharp eye for human foibles, in one of her very perceptive and funny-sad songs about a sister of many older brothers says "and I was allowed to clean for them, and cook for them," and described a lifetime of sisterly deference, until the brothers' children grow up. They come to her, and she "is allowed to clean for them and cook for them" and so shows yet another aspect of the same family structure.

However, in families where attempts are made to treat both genders equally, the relationship between brothers and sisters may be extremely competitive, in a way traditionally recognized as normal between brothers or between sisters, but not usually across the gender line.

All these factors, and others that are unique to individual families, act together to mold the lives of the children of the family, not only during their young years when they live together, but long after when the children are grown up.

The Smith family consists of four offspring, Jessica and Anna, the older two, and Cyril and Irving, the younger ones. The parents had been close and happy together from the start of their marriage, although in fact it had been one into which the couple had been maneuverd by their respective parents. They were financially comfortable and owned a delicatessen.

Jessica was from the first adored by her father, and by the time she was three and her sister Anna was born she had become an imperious child who manipulated her father easily, but had some difficulty pleasing her mother, who tended to be rather strict in her handling of the child.

Anna, in her turn, became Jessica's willing slave, and when Cyril was born when the girls were aged five and two she showed little anxiety about being supplanted as the baby. However, Jessica took Cyril's birth very badly, because the two sets of grandparents (both of whom had had their origins in Central Europe) were male worshipers to a marked degree. They fussed and celebrated over the boy's birth with enormous satisfaction.

The new baby was difficult from the start, always crying, hard to feed, never seeming satisfied, and his mother suffered from depression for the first and only time in her life. By the time he was two his father had taken a strong dislike to the boy, blaming him for his wife's lowness of spirits, an attitude fed by Jessica's constant complaints about him. The only ally Cyril seemed to have was Anna who, young as she was, was considered the only one who could pacify him when he was upset.

The youngest son was born late, when Jessica was ten, Anna seven and Cyril five. Jessica was now of an age to find the new baby adorable, and she became very attached to him in a way that made her and her mother much closer. The mother too adored the baby, for he was easy, fed well, cried little and seemed to have a sunny disposition. The two of them, aided and abetted by Anna (although she remained Cyril's "special one") fussed over Irving constantly. He showed little of the traditional spoiled child behavior, however, because of his easy personality. The father remained rather aloof from the boy, still relating best to Jessica.

Over their growing years these brother-sister relationships became more settled, with Jessica and Anna being reasonably close over "feminine" matters – they shared a room and some clothes, being much the same size – while each related closely to her own "special brother." The boys shifted back and forth from closeness to being at each other's throats, and there were occasional episodes when Cyril was severely punished for being rough with young Irving, though never was Irving punished for similar offences. But even so, by the time the boys reached young adulthood they were on reasonable terms, and it was the younger who acted as the older's protector, source of loans and general support in times of trouble.

It was when the four of them established their adult life patterns that the effects of their childhood brother-sister relationships as molders of their futures could be most clearly seen.

Jessica married a quiet young man, a hard-working, easygoing grocer, amenable to being alternately bossed or pampered. He had much in common with Irving and indeed the brothers-in-law have become great friends. Jessica had one child, a son, after several years of marriage, and she refused to have any more on the grounds of her "poor health," although it is in fact excellent. The son, fortunately for Jessica, is very like his father and uncle in disposition and developed a close relationship with his mother, who repeated her style of care with him. At the time of writing, he is a young man of nineteen and attending a university. He told his mother two years ago that he was homosexual, news she received with more equanimity than her husband did. However, the family remains on reasonably good terms.

Anna married very late, having remained at home to look after her father, who developed hypertension and a heart condition in his late middle age, shortly after his wife's death from breast cancer. He had wanted Jessica to look after him, but she pleaded her marital responsibilities and also her distress at her father's illness. She couldn't see him every day – it would be too upsetting. In fact, since Jessica's husband was well off and she had ample domestic staff she could easily have performed this task for her father, but he accepted her refusal as inevitable and Anna took over. His doctor was often angered by the way the old man would criticize Anna and eulogize Jessica, whom the doctor, having known the family for many years, regarded as "bone selfish."

When the old man died Anna herself got married, to a man considerably her senior and also in frail health. She had wanted children but was deterred by the need to take care of her husband. Also, Cyril had moved in with her soon after her marriage, following one of his many crises (see below). Her husband died within a few years, and Anna never remarried, but continued to look after Cyril. They were badly off since Cyril worked only occasionally, and Anna's husband had not left much. All their father's money had been left to Jessica. She, as the richest member of the family, occasionally provided extras for Anna, but only when Cyril was away from her house. She said she wasn't wasting her money on the likes of him.

Cyril married a lively, very attractive girl after a

short courtship when they were both barely nineteen. They had three children in quick succession, all girls. Cyril's wife became very depressed, partly as a result of post-birth problems but also because of the family's poverty. They lurched from one financial crisis to another, depending entirely on Cyril's erratic earnings as a barber. Once or twice Cyril tried decidedly shady methods to make some cash, since his father and his rich older sister both flatly refused to do anything for him or his family. When he was actually sent to prison for three months his wife left him, taking the children back to her parents. It was at this point he moved in with Anna. He was always a dapper, well-fed looking man, spending most of his time gambling with a coterie of gambling cronies. He never saw or heard from his wife or children after they left him, and he seems not to care.

Irving married well – a strong-minded young woman from a prosperous family, well off and intelligent. With her money they started a dress store which is successful, and now has a second branch. They have two children, a son and a daughter (which Cyril says is "just like Irving – always does what's expected of him, and does it the right way"), both of whom are now at a university, but not the same one as their cousin. Irving's wife, while accepting the closeness between her family and that of Jessica prefers that her own two children should not come under any sort of "bad influence" from him. Little is said on the subject, but Jessica makes sure that her son is never at home when her brother and sister-in-law visit, and she rarely talks about him to the couple – although she discusses him with Irving alone when she gets the chance. The sisters-in-law are in fact uneasy together, and the atmosphere between them is a little strained. But as long as the two men are around, all seems well enough.

Anna has recently been diagnosed as suffering from breast cancer, and her prognosis is poor. Cyril has already approached his brother Irving about his own future, anxious about what will happen to him when Anna dies. "I'm not the sort of man to live alone. And you'll be the only family I've got who cares. Jessica wouldn't cross the road to help me," he says pitifully. Irving, easygoing as ever, is prepared to offer his brother a home, but is having problems with his wife, who loathes Cyril. This is the only area of agreement she has with her sister-in-law Jessica. Just what will happen when Anna dies is hard to say. It seems likely, however, that the two women, Jessica and Irving's wife, will persuade Irving to shrug off his brother's demands on him. What will then happen to Cyril no one can imagine. He has been looked after all his life, and it seems unlikely that he will be capable of coping with self-responsibility at all.

It was gender rather than sex as such which played the major part in the way this family of brothers and sisters have operated over the years and will no doubt operate in the future. Sex, however, seemed to play little part in their relationship. But in others it plays a very large part indeed, as the next case histories will show.

Lena and Thomas were the children of a widow. Their father had died when Lena was three and Thomas two. When they were fifteen and fourteen respectively Lena became pregnant but hid the fact until four months had passed, when she became ill at school and was seen by the school doctor and diagnosed. She was sent to a school counselor and said the reason she had told no one was "because you'd have made me have an abortion." The counselor assured her that no one could force her to have an abortion against her will, and offered to tell her mother about her state in order to help her out. But Lena became hysterical and threatened to kill herself if anyone went to see her mother. Since the school knew the mother was in poor health, and also not very intelligent, it was agreed that Lena's wish should be honored. They would try to arrange for her to go away for a while and would tell some story or other that would satisfy her mother.

This was arranged, and the mother was told by the school counselor that Lena had the chance to go on a special course for a while, and she accepted this. A feckless as well as a stupid woman, she had never shown much concern for her children, who had lived with her in a very haphazard fashion in their extremely squalid home. She seemed quite pleased to be rid of Lena for a while.

Lena remained at school, living at home, until the seventh month of her pregnancy. The staff provided her with full-skirted clothes, and her state remained unsuspected by the majority of teachers and students; she was a solidly built girl, not very attractive, and was given to eating as much chocolate as she could get. If anyone noticed any change in her, they probably put it down to an increase in weight.

Lena then went to the "special course," in fact a mother and baby home in a nearby town. The school staff relaxed, glad to have got her away from home before any crisis developed, and Lena was left to the care of the home's staff. They would arrange for adoption and return Lena to school in due course, her secret well kept.

But, in fact, trouble then began in earnest. Thomas, who had been disregarded by the staff in all the arrangements made for Lena, became very violent about a week after Lena had left, and after a playground scuffle with another boy in which he had so injured the other boy that he had suffered a concussion, he had been brought to the same school counselor. He refused to talk to her; he was truculent, abusive, and showed signs of being altogether out of control. This was puzzling because he had always seemed a very average boy – far from angelic and very low in achievement, but not violent or disruptive like this.

It was almost by accident that the counselor remembered that Thomas was Lena's brother. She asked him if he were worried about Lena, and at this he became even more abusive and showed threatening behavior to the extent of throwing a heavy paperweight through the window, breaking the glass. In the ensuing fuss the police were called, and the boy had to be restrained.

He was then taken to the school doctor, who gave him a large dose of tranquillizers. Not until then could he be handled at all safely – he was a large, well-developed boy, having passed puberty early – and he was then admitted to the hospital. Here, after some time, he was able to establish some rapport with a psychiatrist, and his story emerged.

Unlike Lena, who was of average intelligence, and with a happier environment could have been higher than average in achievement, Thomas was below average. He had been driven to his violent episode by an acute anxiety about his sister, who had, it seemed to him, disappeared. Clearly the pair were very close, and Thomas was very dependent on her, but not until the psychiatrist had talked to the boy several times was it clear just how close they were.

Lena had reached puberty at the age of ten but had not told her mother she was menstruating. She learned how to cope from advertisements she saw in drug stores. She had sent Thomas in to buy what she needed, using money she stole from other children at school.

The two had always shared a bed in a room on their

own (their mother, said Thomas, had her own room because she often had visitors). As far as the psychiatrist could work out, they had shared erotic play from a very early age, with Lena teaching the slower Thomas to touch her genitals and "make me feel nice." This continued after Lena reached puberty, but now Thomas began to find he enjoyed the games as much as Lena did. She no longer had to bribe him with candy (bought with stolen money again) to do it.

Whether the boy's own early onset of puberty was to an extent triggered by these early sexual games was hard to say, but it seemed possible, the psychiatrist later reported, because by the time Thomas was twelve his genitalia were almost fully developed ("same as I am now," Thomas had answered when asked how much he'd changed from two years ago). He, in his turn, had taught Lena to help him masturbate, and the pair reached the stage of having complete intercourse about a year before Lena became pregnant. They had sex about five times a week, with Thomas becoming more and more demanding. It was then his turn to steal money for Lena – he had to offer her bribes.

Her "disappearance" had caused him considerable anxiety, since no one had told him she was going. When his sexual frustration had boiled over, violence had resulted.

In this case, a family of limited intelligence and low income and aspirations had created an environment in which incest might be seen as an inevitable result – but it must never be thought that only "lower-class" people behave in this way. It can happen in "respectable" middle class families as well.

Simon and Sarah were the children of an airline pilot and his physiotherapist wife. They lived in a large, very comfortable house in the suburbs and had a daily housekeeper because their mother worked full time. Until Sarah, the younger child, was eleven, they had a resident nanny. Both children attended expensive private day schools, although the father would have preferred his son to go to his own old boarding school. Their mother, however, was strongly opposed to this. She felt that home was where children ought to be at the end of the day. She made every effort to be at home when the children returned from school so that they would not be "damaged" in any way by having a working mother.

Until Simon was thirteen the parents always asked the housekeeper to babysit when they went out for the evening, but Simon objected at this age, saying it was "babyish." And after a couple of times when they went no further than a neighbor's house, the parents agreed to do without sitters.

They went out about twice a week, always leaving a phone number where they could be reached. Both parents were anxious not to be overprotective, while at the same time they were equally concerned to provide adequate care and security for their children.

The children themselves were close and happy. Because the schools they attended were a long way from their home, there were few school friends they could see after school. Other local children either went to other schools or were uninterested in making friends. Their mother had tried to find local youth clubs for them, but there were none that seemed suitable. (The only two, even in this prosperous area, were "fast" in the mother's view, and it was true that the youngsters who belonged to them tended to drink alcohol a good deal, and, it was suspected, smoked marijuana.) So Simon and Sarah were thrown very much on each other for companionship. But they did not seem at all bothered by this, preferring each other's company even when other children were available – for example, when school friends came to stay for the weekend.

Simon, a big, cheerful boy, was lively and athletic, enjoying riding, swimming and similar physical activities. Sarah was more timid but greatly admired Simon's prowess at sports.

When the children were sixteen and fourteen Sarah, far from being a fat girl, decided to go on a diet and lost weight at an alarming rate. Her mother was worried and, with her medical knowledge, suspected anorexia nervosa. She took Sarah to a psychiatrist and the diagnosis was confirmed, so Sarah began to attend psychotherapeutic sessions.

Simon became very anxious about his sister and extra protective, which comforted the parents a great deal. They felt he might be able to persuade Sarah to eat, when they and the psychiatrist failed. On the psychiatrist's advice they placed themselves in the background as much as they could, making an effort to go out as much as they always had in the evenings, leaving Simon in charge.

Sarah, however, became worse and worse and eventually, weighing less than 70 lb (she was 5 ft 4 in tall), she was admitted to the hospital. There, under intensive psychotherapy and with abreaction techniques (using a judicious combination of drugs and hypnotherapy), she talked, and the story emerged.

One evening when Simon was fourteen and she was twelve they had been alone in the house while their parents were at a play. Sarah was then reaching puberty, and her breasts had begun to develop. Simon had started to tease her about this. He had begun to chase her around the room, pretending he was going to pull her sweater off and look at her breasts, and she, shrieking, had run away and locked herself in a closet.

Eventually he had enticed her out and hugged her, and he said he wouldn't tease her again.

But this episode seemed to have started them off on a pattern of behavior. The romping around and pretending to pull off the sweater happened again several times, and Sarah began to retaliate by trying to pull off Simon's pants to see his "whiskers" (she had accidentally seen him in his bath and noticed that his pubic hair was growing).

Each time the romps would end in hugs, kisses and apologies. And then one night the kissing had got out of hand, become more intense, and Simon had an orgasm. This both alarmed and exhilarated him, and he tried on successive occasions to make it happen again. When kissing didn't seem adequate, he asked his sister to touch his penis to help him. She was both frightened and fascinated by this, and after a while she consented to do it. Simon again climaxed rapidly, and this time Sarah saw it. She was very upset and cried a great deal. "I don't know why," she told the doctor. "I don't know why."

Simon, wanting to make her comfortable and happy again, told her he knew how to make her feel nice, too. He had been told by boys at school and read about it in books, and after a lot of persuasion Sarah had allowed him to touch her vulva. By this time she was in a very emotional state and was clearly aroused, and despite Simon's inexpert approach she had an orgasm herself. She denied to the psychiatrist ever having masturbated to orgasm, but she obviously knew about the possibility. "The girls at school . . ." she said.

The psychiatrist decided not to tell the parents what he had discovered. There seemed little point in distressing them with information they did not, at this stage, need. But they were advised to allow Sarah to go away to a boarding school.

This was agreed, and Simon then asked if he could do the same. So the two went to separate boarding schools, and at the time of writing Sarah is taking university entrance exams. Her weight is stable, but she still needs supervision over her eating habits, and she still resists allowing her weight to rise above 90 lb. But at least her anorexia is under control. Her parents know that the condition is a resistant one, and it may be many years before the word "cure" can be used with any confidence, but they are reasonably hopeful about the future. Simon is now at a university, living in a dormitory, and he spends his summer vacations traveling with friends or on projects of his own. The family accepts the fact that he has now grown up and gone his own way.

Anorexia nervosa, the so-called "dieting disease," has been said to have different triggers. Some psychiatrists see it as a form of food phobia, others as due to an organic disturbance involving brain function, yet others as a form of denial of sexuality. The anorexic girl (the disease is most common in girls) loses her breasts, stops menstruating and becomes very childlike in figure. The psychiatrist in charge of Sarah's case says that in his experience problems with the parental relationship usually lie behind this sort of anorexia nervosa, but a complicated relationship with a sibling can clearly have the same effect. He suspects that Sarah's root problem was her own ambivalent feelings. She both enjoyed and feared her own as well as her brother's sexuality. The retreat into anorexia removed the conflict, by removing her sexual characteristics.

Sexual tension between brother and sister will not always show in an obviously sexual manner. Sometimes there will be behavior that has a symbolic sexual significance.

Diane and Gerald were twins, born to lively, intelligent and very cosmopolitan parents fairly late in their marriage. There were no other children. The twins were very much alike and were always happy in each other's company, though they displayed almost stereotyped gender orientation quite early in life: Diane was always rather deferential toward Gerald, while he was always rather lordly and protective toward her. But that they loved each other dearly was never in any doubt.

There were no problems at all during their growing years, and both weathered puberty happily. Then Diane met and fell in love with Charles, a highly intelligent and capable young man. It wasn't an easy courtship – Charles was not certain at first about how much he wanted to commit himself to marriage, but Diane, perhaps a little uncharacteristically, was adamant that this was the man she wanted and pursued him with some determination. She first had intercourse with him about a year before they decided to get engaged, and this sexual relationship continued.

Apart from this slightly unconventional behavior (this was during the early 1960s, before sexual "permissiveness" had become the norm), the couple behaved otherwise in a very ordinary way: they announced their engagement, found an apartment and furnished it, then had an elegant wedding and set off for a European honeymoon.

A key to the brand-new apartment with its brand-new furniture was left with the twins' parents while the newlyweds were away, in case of emergencies. One night a couple of days after the wedding Gerald borrowed the key and took a casual girlfriend to the apartment, where he slept with her in his sister's and brother-in-law's new bed. He made no attempt to tidy up the next day, but left it crumpled.

When Diane returned to her new home with her new husband and discovered what Gerald had done she was extremely distressed. She confronted Gerald, who could not understand what all the fuss was about; hadn't she been "screwing around" before she married her Charles? He refused to take her objection to what she regarded as a personal violation with any seriousness. A coolness developed between brother and sister that has continued to this day.

They are now on friendly terms, but there is no special "closeness" of the sort that had been so important to both of them when they were younger. Gerald is now married, but Diane dislikes her sister-in-law and is particularly incensed by what she regards as her intense competitiveness. Whatever Diane does, such as going into analysis (when she discovered just why she had been so angered by Gerald's behavior that night in her new apartment), taking a psychology or art history course, or whatever, her sister-in-law copies.

Diane now knows that her brother's action was undoubtedly a sexual one; that by having sex with another girl in his sister's marriage bed before she and her husband had shared it themselves he had symbolically had sex with his sister before her husband had. The fact that the couple had enjoyed an active sex life for some time was unimportant; it was the newness of the bed and the apartment that was significant to Gerald.

Sexual rivalry between siblings does not always cross the gender barrier. It is also possible for same-sex children to develop strong sexual feelings for each other, which later express themselves as intense rivalry.

Violet and Edith were born just ten months apart. Both

their parents worked long hours in their small newspaper and confectionery shop and the girls spent a
great deal of their time together and were inseparable
by the time they were four and five years old. They even
started school together, the younger girl being allowed
to start early to avoid separation from her sister.

Throughout their primary school days they remained
close, each sister jealously excluding anyone else
from their relationship. After they started high school,
however, Violet, the older sister, began to pull away
and seemed ready to have other friends and relationships, much to Edith's rage and distress. But Violet
persisted and there were many scenes and fights because Edith meddled in Violet's private affairs – sending anonymous notes to her school friends, hanging
around when Violet wanted to be alone with a boy she
had brought home, spying on her whenever she could,
and so on.

The parents took Violet's side in these fights and
insisted that Edith also make her own friends, but she
never did.

Violet married an old school friend when she was
twenty-three, after working for a while with her sister
and parents in their business. Edith became very ill
just before the wedding, developing such severe abdominal pain that she was admitted to the hospital to
have a laparotomy – an exploratory operation – the
night before, which put quite a damper on the celebrations. She was found to have no abdominal abnor-
malities and made a good recovery.

The following year Edith married a rather shy young
man she had met only a few weeks earlier when he
delivered some parcels to the family store. She swept
him off his feet, in fact. Her wedding was much more
expensive and splendid than Violet's had been, but this
time Violet missed the family celebration, because she

had had a miscarriage the week before and was unable to leave her bed.

Violet went on having obstetric problems and lost two more pregnancies; she then developed acute abdominal pain, was rushed to the hospital and operated on for an ectopic pregnancy. Her right fallopian tube had to be removed, and she was very ill as she suffered from peritonitis afterwards. This peritonitis also resulted in severe inflammation of the remaining fallopian tube, and as a result Violet was told she was unable to have any children of her own. She and her husband then set about arranging for adoption. In time they adopted three children.

Meanwhile Edith had become very distressed over her sister's poor health and was a devoted visitor and nurse, leaving her husband to work in the store, which they had now taken over from her elderly parents. Everyone was touched to see how much love and care Edith lavished on her ailing sister. The only person who seemed less than impressed was Jack, Violet's husband. He and Edith had never liked each other, and when Violet became ill the antipathy between them increased.

When Violet was well again and her first adopted baby had joined the family, Edith became pregnant. The pregnancy was normal, though Edith complained of feeling ill almost all the time, and she was delivered of a healthy son. But she said that the labor had been so dreadful an experience that she would never have another child, not on any account. Her suffering had been intense and so agonizing that she could not, she said, ever be expected to go through such a thing again.

Throughout this period Violet spent a lot of time visiting her sister and being very supportive, much to Jack's irritation. Then, when the baby was only two weeks old and after Edith had been home from the hospital for only one day, the baby was found dead in his crib. The doctors diagnosed the "Sudden Infant Death" syndrome – "crib death." No obvious cause was identified at the postmortem.

Three months later Edith adopted a daughter by using the services of a "black market" adoption agency. She had been turned down by every reputable agency she had approached because she was not, in fact, infertile and could have had a child of her own. But she continued to say she would never have her own child because she could not face such physical anguish again.

At the time of writing, Edith is going through the process of adopting her fourth child. Violet is said to be considering acquiring a fourth as well, if she can find one.

The parallels in the behavior of these two sisters need no underlining. But in considering the whole question of brother/sister relationships, as well as brother/brother and sister/sister, some important points do need emphasizing.

The fact that a pair of young people are related as closely as siblings are does not preclude them from feeling stirrings of sexual interest in each other. The taboo on erotic contact between brothers and sisters is not based on biological imperatives but on intellectual decisions. In other species there is no built-in prevention of mating between siblings. Nor need there be.

The most common reason given for the objection to such mating among humans is that it produces damaged offspring. Yet, in fact, we deliberately breed animals in this way in order to improve a bloodline and to create the characteristics we "lords of the planet" have decided we want those animals to bear. If such breeding is satisfactory for animals, is there any reason why it shouldn't be all right for us?

In ancient times, in fact, it was encouraged. The royal house of Egypt maintained its dynastic control on the country by close intermarriage within the family. The Ptolemys always married their sisters – no one else was thought to be of sufficiently high blood for them! And European royal families interbred closely for many years, not brothers and sisters admittedly, but siblings' offspring. Many were the sprigs of the princehood who, themselves the offspring of first cousins, then married their own first cousins.

That this led to the spread of hemophilia through the courts of Europe (it seems Queen Victoria was the first carrier) is true. It is also true that it was a first-cousin marriage between two members of a closely inbred aristocratic family which produced a child who suffered from the hereditary disease of osteogenesis imperfecta – the "brittle bone" syndrome. (In this the bones fracture easily and often, heal poorly, and the eventual result is loss of stature with severe deformity.) That child became a remarkable painter – the family were the Counts of Toulouse Lautrec.

But, in both these cases, families which had interbred for many generations were involved. A first-time brother/sister liaison which resulted in a child would not necessarily mean that child would be genetically damaged.

The taboo on incest is as likely to be based on an ancient hunger for wealth and land as on any real anxiety about genetic problems. When a man's son chose a wife from another family or tribe, he brought back with this new person new money and possessions with which to enrich the whole family. When a daughter chose or was given to an outside partner, she took herself away to be fed at another man's table. If a man's offspring married each other, what was there in it for the patriarch and through him the tribe? Nothing at all.

There are good reasons why children who have grown up together should find each other sexually attractive. Propinquity, for a start. While for some it is true that a new face, a new smell or a new sound in a voice are attractive because they are exotic, the vast majority of us are attracted by the familiar because it makes us feel most comfortable.

It is no accident that so many couples who love each other enough to marry share a physical resemblance. In people who have been married for many years the likeness may be due in part to the sharing of experience and the mimicry that we all use – but it can be seen even in some comparatively new couples. They chose each other because they look alike. And brothers and sisters can look very alike.

Community of interest is also important. When you share not only a common language but common assumptions, attitudes and ideas, having derived them from the same source, you are likely to find each other sexually attractive as well.

It is very interesting that people of the Victorian and Edwardian ages were very aware of this fact, as is shown in much fiction of those periods. Brothers were held up to sisters as ideals of manhood, and men were expected to regard their sisters as so very sexually desirable and therefore vulnerable that they needed constant vigilance. When Lytton Strachey was taken to court during World War I because he had a conscientious objection to fighting in the army, he was asked what he would do "if a German soldier tried to rape your sister." This was regarded as the acid test. (Actually he answered flippantly, "I would interpose my body," which caused a great stir, since his homosexuality was a matter of some concern. But that's another story.)

In practice, as we all know, most people are not sexually drawn to their siblings. I suspect that the most likely reason for this is that most of us are flung apart, rather than drawn together, by our shared family experience. Unresolved jealousies dating from infancy (and by the way, younger children can be jealous of older ones, seeing them as tyrants, just as much as older ones can resent younger ones as intruders) and the succeeding years of sibling rivalry can have a repelling effect.

The taboo is still so powerful, and there is still such anxiety about young sexuality, that the average parent goes to some trouble to keep opposite-sex siblings well separated. (So does authority: in Britain people who rent public housing can ask to be moved to an apartment with an extra bedroom if there is any risk that opposite-sex children will have to share – even while they are quite young.)

This leads to what could be regarded as an amusing anomaly. Opposite-sex children are protected by their parents, sometimes consciously, sometimes not, from the risk of sharing erotic play which might lead to actual incest. Yet despite the widespread publicity about the incidence of homosexuality and the (I believe) absurd fear and repugnance of it many people have, it is rare, if ever, that parents concern themselves about the possibility of erotic play between same-sex siblings. Yet, if brothers and sisters are at risk of sharing sex unless they are supervised, aren't brothers and brothers, sisters and sisters, also?

There is in fact some evidence that plenty of brothers have gained some of their sex education – that is, knowledge of how their own bodies work – by sharing masturbatory play with each other, and plenty of girls have also played sex games with their nearest and most available playmates – their sisters. I discovered this for myself by asking adults I know what they had done during their own childhoods. I asked about 130 people – not really a statistical sample, perhaps, but a fair number – and ninety-eight of them had such memories. And they all seem to be reasonably well-balanced heterosexuals now.

However, sometimes a childhood sexual liaison can persist well into adult life and create complex problems for the individuals concerned.

Daphne and Cecily were born in a small town in Vermont seven years apart around the turn of the century. Three other children came between them, two boys and a girl, but Daphne was the oldest and Cecily the youngest. They were the children of a family doctor and as such part of the local elite. They were "rich" and brought up to be aloof from the "ordinary" children of the town. They were provided with a governess to teach them, rather than going to the local school because this was considered more genteel by their socially conscious parents.

The two brothers, who were close in childhood and excluded their sisters, were sent away to expensive boarding schools at the ages of ten and eleven, and thereafter they and their sisters were remote from each other. The remaining sister died of scarlet fever at the beginning of World War I, and their mother never recovered from the shock of this death. She died in a post-war epidemic of Spanish influenza when Daphne and Cecily were nineteen and twelve respectively. The brothers, now aged eighteen and seventeen, went away to college and never lived in the family home again. Only the two sisters and their aging, difficult father were left. He had become very withdrawn and irascible after his daughter's and his wife's deaths, and the girls were thrown together even more.

The old doctor retired from active practice in 1948, and the family no longer had as much money as they once did. But the daughters went on as they always had, spending all their time together, looking after their old father and seeming content enough. They had few friends, and were seen shopping in the town once a week, always taking it in turns, while the other remained home with the now-bedridden old father. Visitors, old friends of the family in its younger years, were discouraged, and anyway died off as the years went on.

The old doctor died in 1976 at the age of ninety-six, having been totally blind, deaf and apparently senile for many years, and for the first time for many years outsiders had access to the old house. Daphne was now aged seventy-six and her sister was sixty-nine. The young local doctor and his nurse, Mary, arrived when Daphne frantically went to see them after years of apparently not needing medical care, to announce her father's death. They were distressed by what they found when they went to the house. It was still tolerably well furnished, but it had become appallingly dirty, though the women themselves seemed clean enough.

After the old man's body had been removed and the formalities dealt with, the nurse Mary tried to help the "poor old dears," as she called them. She wanted to visit regularly, to arrange for local voluntary organizations to provide meals, domestic help and so on, but there were difficulties. Daphne, the older, was suspicious and hostile and rejected all advances, slamming the door in Mary's face whenever she called, and doing the same to the young doctor, who was equally concerned.

The doctor gave up eventually, but Mary did not. She still tried to make contact, but each time, when she rang the doorbell, Cecily answered it, and then scuttled away as Daphne came furiously to throw the door shut again.

But Mary thought that Cecily seemed less difficult than her sister, so she watched for her in town and realized that they were still doing as they always had – that was, taking the shopping in turn, even though there was no one left to look after in the old house.

One day she approached Cecily and found, as she had suspected, that she was quite willing to be friendly. In fact, she blossomed into quite a chatterbox given the chance! She talked a lot, over cups of coffee at a local coffee shop, about her childhood and how it had been in the old days "before the war" (World War I, Mary soon realized!), and how nice it had all been. But mention of her sister made her tense and worried, and she would scuttle away home whenever Mary mentioned her. So she stopped.

Then winter came and Mary noticed that neither old lady had appeared in town for two weeks. Anxious for Cecily, of whom she had become quite fond, she braved Daphne's wrath and went visiting.

She found them both ill, having had to break a window to get in when there was no answer to the bell. They had caught pneumonia in the icy house. Daphne had to be admitted to the hospital, she was so severely affected, but it was thought that Cecily could recover at home with good nursing, which Mary was willing to provide. She moved into the house temporarily.

The old woman and the young one now became much closer friends. Mary's own mother had died some years earlier, and she felt a warmth for this nice old lady which made Cecily even more garrulous. Mary began to realize that Daphne had a very close control over her younger sister.

How close she did not realize until Daphne came

home, weak but recovered from her pneumonia. Within two days she had made so much fuss about Mary's presence in the house that Cecily begged her to go, and there was a considerable argument. Daphne accused the younger woman of having designs on their money (which was manifestly absurd, since the house and its contents were all they owned and none of it was worth very much), and Cecily wept and became quite distraught at Daphne's behavior.

So Mary had to leave, but she was worried and upset enough to contact the local welfare office and ask them to intervene. She said she feared for the old ladies' welfare, with no one to look after them.

The welfare people were unwilling to interfere. They said that the doctor would have to request their involvement, so Mary went to the doctor, by now very much concerned, to ask him to do so. He thought Mary was getting overinvolved with the situation, and said so, trying to help Mary see that she was trying to replace her own mother by getting so tied up with Cecily. Mary was very distressed by this and talked a lot to the doctor, meanwhile agreeing to keep away from the old ladies and their house.

Three weeks later Mary told the doctor that again she had not seen either of the sisters in town and was worried about them, and this time he went to visit the house.

Again there was no answer to the doorbell and he had to break in. The two old ladies were found dead in the same bed, having swallowed all of the sleeping tablets that Daphne had been given by the doctors at the hospital.

Mary was so upset by this that the doctor thought she needed psychotherapy and arranged it. It was during discussions with her therapist that her feelings emerged. The therapist's analysis, which Mary eventu-

ally accepted as accurate, was that the sisters had
developed a relationship that was certainly as intense
and as important to them as any sexual tie, even if
there had been no actual sexual contact (and no one
could ever know now whether there had been). Daphne
had reacted to the threat that she thought Mary posed
to her relationship with all the classic behavior of
sexual jealousy. Their suicide pact underlined the
power of this close relationship.

Mary needed many months of psychiatric help to
recover from what had been, for her, a very traumatic
experience. She is now back at work, though not in the
same town, and has formed a close relationship with
another much older woman, with whom she shares an
apartment. Her own tendency to homosexual feeling is
becoming clearer and adds another level of understanding to the relationship between the elderly
sisters. They had been aware of her need and her
deeper reasons for getting involved with them, even if
they had not been able to put it into words.

One of the most interesting aspects of this situation is
that at no point did society – the neighbors – ever
point any disapproving fingers at the sisters. Their
relationship, if it were thought about at all, was seen
by outsiders as a sentimentally sweet attachment between two loving sisters. Yet clearly there was much
more to it than that. There often is, in sibling relationships.

11
The Adolescent Explosion

KERRY AGED FIVE: "Being grown up means having ice cream any time you want it. It means sitting on your own special chair that no one else can sit in and telling children to be good all the time."

Kerry's Mother: "What sort of adult will she be? Lovely, I think. She's such a charming child now – so willing and helpful."

James, aged nine: "When I'm grown up I'll live in a house in the forest that I'll build out of wood and things I find there and I'll catch my own food, rabbits and things, with snares or by running after them, even, and I'll have a wood fire and no one'll ever know I'm there on my own."

James's Father: "Listen, unless he changes some of his ways, he won't have *any* sort of life as an adult. Try to get him to take schoolwork seriously and you break your head. Try to get him to keep himself even half clean and you end up screaming. He's so damned thoughtless, that kid."

Barbara, aged twelve: "I'm already grown up, only they won't let me be. I mean, I think a lot, and I'm serious about things and I've had my periods for nearly a year and I've got a 34-in bust, bigger than anyone else in my class. I'm already grown up."

Barbara's Mother: "I think about it often. She'll have lovely children and everyone will say to me, 'How can you be a grandmother, you don't look old enough to have children old enough to be married,' and they'll all be as jealous as hell."

Andrew, aged fifteen: "I don't want to grow up. I really don't. It's good enough as it is except for all the damned studying I have to do. I've got a girl friend now and we get a thrill out of each other and it's fun, but grown up – responsibilities, you know? Worrying about money, how to bring up your children – I don't want it to happen. But it damn well will, won't it?"

Andrew's Mother: "Andrew, a man? I try to see it, but all I can imagine is looking up at Andrew as I know him. Tall and big, but still Andrew with ink on his ears."

Father of four: "How will it be when the kids are grown up? Cheaper."

There is a period in a child's life which is regarded by many parents as the Best; the years that come after infancy and toddlerhood are past, and before adolescence starts.

"It's great right now – they don't wake us up in the middle of the night to be fed or to pee, and we don't lie awake till the small hours wondering what the hell time they're coming home."

The years that run between, say, four or five and twelve or thirteen can be comfortable and satisfying in many ways for both parents and children. They have had time to get to know each other, and to recognize – even, possibly to understand – each other's personalities; they have identified each other's idiosyncrasies and have probably developed a pattern of living – "this is the way we do things in this family" – and the lines of authority are clearly defined.

It is a short period, barely ten years or so in a child's lifetime, yet over and over again parents tend to behave as though the child will be as it is during this time for eternity. Oh, they pay lip service to the idea of The Future; they worry about the children's schooling because of the need to get into the Right university, which is vital for the Right career, and so on – but they rarely if ever think of a time when their children will no longer be the children they now know. When they visualize The Future they somehow see their children merely as larger versions of the way they are at present, not as adults who will be quite different physically, emotionally and intellectually.

It is because parents have such difficulty absorbing the fact that their children will change as they become adults that the period of change – adolescence – is so often painful for both them and their offspring. It ought to be easy for parents to understand what it is like to make the uneasy journey from one state to the other; they've been through it themselves, after all. But adult life seems to bring with it an amnesia for the transition period. Generation after generation of parents make the same mistakes in living with their growing children, create the same arguments, stir up the same agonies.

And for the same reasons. Many of the miseries of the adolescent period are based on the fear of loss. Children fear the loss of their childhood, viewing the future as adults with apprehension. They need a lot of support and encouragement to let go of the one and welcome the other. But the people from whom the support should come – the parents – are themselves suffering from a fear of loss – the loss of their babies, the loss of the satisfactions that come from having a living creature dependent on you, the loss of the prestige enjoyed by the parents of young children; above all, the loss of their own youth. For an adult to be born, a child must die, and when that child dies, the parents' young lives die with him/her.

When Wordsworth wrote in *Ode on Intimations of Immortality*, "Heaven lies about us in our infancy, shades of the prison house begin to close upon the growing boy," he was writing only of children. But it is a much more poignant truth for the parents of the child. The growth of a child in fact brings intimations of mortality – the seeds of their own death. Glory for themselves can only be in their children's babyhood. So who can blame parents if they try to hold back time and stop adolescence from happening?

But of course they can't; and the way it happens and the ways both parents and children deal with it vary enormously.

It has been repeated over and over in these pages that individual circumstances cause variations, that personalities, finances and cultural backgrounds as well as gender differences all have an enormous effect on the patterns individual families create, and the solutions they find – or fail to find – for their problems. Never is this more true than in the adolescent period. The adolescent experience will display clearly the effects of the way the family handled past experiences.

Take the matter of toilet training. Considering how basic and normal a matter it is to empty the bladder and rectum and how comfortably animals deal with excretion, we as a species make rather a lot of fuss over it. Especially in the nice, clean, hygienic West. A runaway best seller in the United States in 1976 was not a book about art, philosophy or religion, or even a book with a damned good story. It was a book about how to train a child to use a toilet within a few hours. To say we are obsessive about excretion is to put it mildly.

It is obvious that this excretory obsession is rooted in sexual obsession. A nineteenth-century Scottish obstetrician used to say mournfully to his students, "Far be it from me to criticize the Good Lord in His Wisdom, but I find myself wondering from time to time why He chose to set the nursery between the sewers." The same idea was expressed more pithily by a medieval commentator: "We are borne between pisse and shytte."

The close anatomical juxtaposition of reproductive and excretory equipment means that every time a human empties bladder or bowels he or she is reminded powerfully of the other functions of that part of their body.

Adults have to be, therefore, as discreet about excretion as they are about copulation – and indeed, there are many of us who would much more happily copulate in front of an audience than be seen squatting on a toilet emptying our bowels. The ultimate in intimacy between two people has been defined not as the sharing of sexual pleasure but the ability to fart in each other's presence.

Infants, on the other hand, are totally lacking in discretion. They are unconcerned about controlling their excretion. At first, of course, they don't even know it happens. Then comes a stage when they enjoy the sensations it creates. And then comes another stage when the adults in their lives move in and insist they do it *their* way.

In practice, a great many adults try to move in on the act long before they are likely to have any effect (it is not until the age of fifteen to eighteen months that a baby's neurological pathways have developed enough to make control of excretion possible). Many mothers, hearing a baby cry, will say confidently, "He's wet – he wants changing," and will change the diaper. When the child then settles down to sleep they assume that they correctly identified the cause of distress. But, in fact, babies do not cry when they pee unless the skin of their buttocks or groin is damaged and the urine stings. A normal, healthy baby couldn't care less about being wet or soiled – but likes being handled. That is why having a diaper changed makes the child settle.

Be that as it may, when toilet training begins in earnest a great many things happen to the child, apart from learning to pee into a pot. Children learn from their mothers how to feel about this "special" area of their body. They will be taught that it is "nice" or "nasty," "clean" or "dirty." They have something to enjoy or something to be ashamed of. And in so learning, they learn their later attitudes to sexuality.

Virtually from the beginning, even the most relaxed of mothers (it's usually mothers who are involved in toilet training) will underline in the child different responses to sex by their handling of the method of training. Handling, literally. A small boy, when he is being taught to use a potty, has to learn to push his penis down inside the pot he is sitting on so that he doesn't pee over the top, or to so arrange himself so that the splash guard on the receptacle prevents the floor from getting wet. Or he may be taught to stand up to pee, and to aim his stream. This means that he is very likely to have his penis handled by his mother as she teaches him. A girl, on the other hand, does not enjoy such handling. (I use the word "enjoy" deliberately.) Her sex is hidden, secret, deep. And if a mother is too uptight to teach her son to stand up and delegates the task to a man, once again the child is handled by an adult in a way that implies that it is permissible to do so. And of course, from childhood on, he legitimately handles his penis himself every time he empties his bladder. A girl is not expected to so handle herself.

She may have been taught to dry her vulva, but certainly not to actually touch it with her bare hands.

What all this means is that long after, when the child reaches the stage of developing sexual awareness in the same body area where once there was only excretory awareness, the reaction to those feelings will be heavily colored by the early emotions and habits created by toilet training.

Nowhere is this more clear than in the matter of masturbation. For a long time now it has been generally accepted that virtually all boys, 99.9 percent, masturbate. Kinsey put the "you'll-get-hairy-hands-and-go-mad" brigade to final flight, though some of its messages are still reverberating in anxious minds around the world, but only for males. His later research allowed that women, too, masturbate, but in markedly smaller numbers. And he was right – to this day, sex therapists report that many of the nonorgasmic women who seek their help (and there are a very large number of them) strongly deny ever having masturbated. And this fact is a large part of their sexual problem: if you've never been able to give yourself an orgasm, how are you ever going to be able to let anyone else do so?

It seems reasonable to suppose that one reason for this bias is that girls are, from toilet training days on, made to feel that directly touching their own genitalia is wrong. Boys are not. So, later on, boys find it possible to discover the joys of masturbation much more easily than girls. I for one doubt very much that girls are naturally less sexy than boys, and that *this* is why fewer of them masturbate in their pubertal years. In fact, it says a lot for girls' sexiness that so many do manage to overcome the touch-not taboo built into them by early potty training experience, and find their own clitoris.

Another childhood experience that strongly colors

the adolescent one is the manner in which discipline is applied. Although for many years enlightened people have been preaching a doctrine of gentle discipline, eschewing corporal punishment and urging a method of rewards for desired behavior rather than chastisement for unwanted behavior, the fact remains that slapping children still goes on much the way it always has. Mostly for boys. A sharp smack on a young male behind has long been regarded as healthy and salutary, while the same attention to a female one as rather peculiar, to say the least.

People who object to such treatment of girls are usually hard put to say why, but if they do manage a reason, it's along the lines that girls are weaker and smaller than boys. Which is of course ridiculous, because a boy of eight is smaller and weaker than a girl of ten, usually, yet he'll get his share of whipping while the girl gets her traditional punishment – removal of privileges, banishment from the family circle for a while, or extra chores or whatever.

The important point about the use of corporal punishment is not so much whether it is effective as a deterrent of future "crime" when compared with the female sort of punishment, as the effect it has on the sufferer. First of all, corporal punishment results in physical sensations, not just emotional ones. They are supposed to be disagreeable, but as we all know, pain can be enjoyed. Consider the way one persists in prodding with the tongue an aching tooth; it hurts to do so, but it is also an interesting experience. There are children who learn very early to enjoy whipping. Victorian pornography with its emphasis on flagellation shows clearly that a considerable number of adults (including intelligent, cultured people, such as the poet Algernon Swinburne) had been trained to be so by childhood discipline.

But there is of course also the matter of psychological responses to punishment. I believe a very significant fact about corporal punishment is that it is more likely *to improve* a child's self-esteem than to damage it, when compared with other methods. Children who are whipped excite sympathy in their peers if they cry or admiration of their courage if they don't, and they feel the same way about themselves. The child who is banished to bed early is much more likely to arouse pity (not at all the same as sympathy or jeers) and feels great shame, self-dislike and no admiration at all, for where's brave in sitting alone and missing your supper? Nowhere.

There is, of course, far more to the discipline than punishment; such matters as what is regarded as good behavior and why, and how long bad behavior is tolerated and why, and the family standards of behavior when compared with those of others. But this much can be said as a general rule: when family standards have been reasonable, that is, within the child's grasp because they are linked to his age and his abilities; where there is a free exchange between parents and children rather than autocratic refusal by their elders to give youngsters a hearing; where boundaries of behavior are clearly set and don't wobble under pressure; where authority is firm and serene rather than domineering – then the need for any sort of punishment is likely to be small, and the children are likely to grow up with enough self-esteem to weather the pains of adolescence. The most painful part of the changes of puberty is that it is often so hard for children to like themselves, to feel that under a possibly unprepossessing exterior (spots, gangliness or pubertal fat) there lies a worthwhile and lovable human being who will emerge one day from this nasty chrysalis. And the wrong sort of discipline can make the pain greater.

The third childhood experience that plays a highly significant part in adolescence is, of course, sex education. If only we were primitive and didn't live in separate rooms in separate houses, how easy it would all be! Our children would see us virtually naked all the time and would have a realistic view of normal adult bodies upon which to base their opinion of their own when they develop. They would see us copulate and give birth and would accept it all as easily as they accept the fact that we eat and walk around.

But we are not primitive, unfortunately, so our children need this specific information-giving process called "sex education." And we in the West are almost as obsessed with it as we are with toilet training. Professors, parents, parsons and politicians talk on and on and on about it, publishing houses grow fat on the profits that come from publishing books about it (some authors don't do too badly, either) as the unending saga of the sperm and ovum is spelled out to succeeding generations of children. The Facts of Sex, the Morality of Sex, the Reasons for Sex – the words whirl around the heads of our hapless young and make the adults pretty dizzy as well.

But what is more important than the Sensible Words in the Sensible Books are the messages which come from parents to children as they discuss the contents of the books, or pass on information about anatomy and physiology without bothering with anyone else's text.

There is the mother who talks about sex to her daughter in such a way that she implies the girl's body is a chalice, carrying some precious jewel at its heart which may be touched only by "one special person." This is the attitude that lies behind the "Sleeping Beauty" myth: the virginal perfection is "awakened" – i.e., given sexual awareness – by the "kiss" – that is, the first experience of intercourse with orgasm – by a unique man – a "prince."

Mothers who sell this particular bill of goods have a tendency to imply that they themselves, despite their maternity, are still unawakened Sleeping Beauties. They talk about sex as though it happens to other women, as though it might, oh dear, happen to their dear daughter, but never of course has it happened to *them*. The mother who can cheerfully tell her daughter that she enjoys her own sexuality, that she enjoyed it outside or before marriage if she actually did, is unusual to say the least. Though possibly, as the Women's Movement and its ideas spread, more women may be able to admit this.

There is a contrast to this sort of mother who is very interesting indeed, and she is the one who seeks to push her daughter into premature sexual activity – premature in the sense that the girl herself does not necessarily feel ready for it. These are the "thoroughly modern mothers" who take their daughters to doctors to have them put on the Pill or some other contraceptive device. The ones who eagerly discuss with their daughters every detail of sexual activity, giving them a sort of crash course in advanced sexual gymnastics.

I am about to state my own prejudice. I see active sexuality – that is, sexual practice shared with another person – as a function of adulthood. Some people reach this stage earlier than others; I have met fourteen-year-old adults and forty-year-old children. But whenever the stage arrives, and a girl or boy feels ready him- or herself for sexuality, I don't believe he/she needs the assistance of a person a great deal older to facilitate its expression. If a girl of fifteen wants contraception, she doesn't, surely, need to trot along to the doctor's holding her mother's hand. Holding her boyfriend's hand, by all means. I am not suggesting that she may not be glad of support in what is for many young people an alarming confrontation. But a boyfriend is entitled to be involved, a parent is not. The sight of masterful mothers sitting in hospital waiting rooms in my nursing days, accompanying daughters who were there to discuss contraception, depressed me.

It seems to me that such mothers are not so much acting out of "thorough modernity" as out of a rather sleazy search for vicarious sexual experience. It is as though they want to share their child's sex life as a way of fulfilling a need of their own. It is dangerous – not for the mother, who gets a great deal of pleasure from it – but for the child. Growing up is about growing away. It is possible and indeed delightful for a newly developed but self-assured adult to return to the relationship that once existed between him- or herself and a parent, and to reestablish it on the basis of *pares inter pares* – equal among equals. An adult relationship in fact, not a dependent, tension-rich, parent-child one. But this cannot be possible until there has been the necessary period of separation. And mothers who insist on sharing a daughter's sex life just don't allow the separation to take place.

And, of course, they do it with sons as well.

Dear Claire,

My son has been looking rather tense, so I talked with him and he admitted that he and his wife are having problems with sex – she just isn't responsive enough and seems to have some sort of barrier across her vagina that makes things very difficult for my son. I have tried to talk to my daughter-in-law, but she is a very chilly girl, and not at all approachable, unlike our family in many ways, for we are very friendly. However, I want to help all the same, and I need to know the name of a good doctor in our area who will operate on her.

How's that for putting the knife in?

It must not be assumed that men do not ever behave in this way with their sons. Indeed, there is a long tradition of this, hallowed by society in the past as "good fathering." Rich men in Britain once commonly took their young adult sons to Paris for their first sexual experience, introducing them to their own favorite brothels for their sexual baptism. A father who did not make such an arrangement was regarded as most lax by his peers. And it is not unusual today for men to tacitly encourage their sons to have recourse to prostitutes for a first experience.

Also, of course, both mothers and fathers may try to block sexual expression in a child of the opposite gender in order to hold that child's sexuality for him- or herself. The father who forbids his daughter to go out with a boy and the mother who frightens off her son's girlfriend aren't being even slightly subtle.

So sex education is more than just a matter of facts or morality. Probably even more significant is the "politics of sex" – and I don't mean the Women's Movement or male chauvinism, though to an extent they come into it. I mean the way parents deal at an unspoken level with their children when talking to them about sex. Or, of course, keeping silent about it. The uptight Calvinist mother who keeps her lips firmly closed and never discusses bodily functions or sexuality with her daughters (let alone her sons) is speaking volumes. Thou shalt not, it's disgusting, yuk, yuk, yuk, comes across loud and clear.

It is not only parents who send out political messages about sexuality to young people. Society as a whole does it via the popular media. Let me return to one of the most fruitful sources of social information, popular song lyrics.

"My momma done tol' me, when I was in knee pants –
a woman's a two-face, a worrisome thing who'll leave
you to sing the blues in the night."

That's a woman talking about women to her pubertal
son: a great message.

"I want a girl, just like the girl who married dear old
dad. She was a pearl, and the only girl that Daddy ever
had."

This young man is successfully brainwashed into
believing his mother to be the ultimate in feminine
perfection – low in sex drive ("a good, old-fashioned
girl with eyes of blue – who loves nobody else but you.")
to match his father's ("the only girl that Daddy ever
had"), with the firm message that that is the best way
to be.

"While playing at a game of golf, I might make a play
for the caddie, but if I do then I don't follow through,
'cos my heart belongs to Daddy."

A lot of complex messages here. Daddy is either a
real father who would object strenuously and cut off
financial support if his virginal little darling did anything so dreadful as have sex with a young man, or a
sugar daddy, a rich man expecting sexual fidelity from
a girl in exchange for financial benefits, who would
object even more strongly. The underlying message is
that either way, what sex offers a girl is primarily
financial benefit – prostitution is the ideal.

A similar song comes from Cole Porter's show *Kiss
Me Kate*: "Mr. Harris, plutocrat, wants to give my
cheek a pat. If a Harris pat means a Paris hat, okay.
But I'm always true to you, darlin', in my fashion."

"A man chases a girl until she catches him . . ."

This one encourages women to see a sexual relationship as the result of scheming on her part, gullibility on his. It is obviously closely linked with the songs above in its essential message.

"Another bride, another groom, another sunny honeymoon, another season, another reason, for makin' whoopee – he doesn't make much money, only two thousand per. Some judge who thinks he's funny says you give three to her."

Which starts with the sweet joys of sex being allowed by getting married, goes on to show what a dreary business marriage turns into when babies arrive, and ends with a grasping wife robbing the poor sap blind with the collusion of an older father-figure. Altogether a very sour warning to men of what misery awaits anyone with a normal sex drive who likes to enjoy himself (make whoopee).

A similar song is "Remember Me": "Do you recall a cottage small upon a hill, where every day I had to pay another bill." And many old musichall numbers: "She told me her age was three and twenty, cash in the bank she had a'plenty. I was the fool who believed it all, I was the M.U.G. At Trinity Church I met my doom, now we live in a top back room – up to my ears in debt for rental – I was her M.U.G."; "She was a dear little dicky bird, tweet, tweet, tweet she went – sweetly she sang to me till all my money was spent – then she went off song and we parted on fighting terms – she was one of the early birds, and I was one of the worms."

Social attitudes like these underlie every individual family's relationships. So do individual psyches. But all the time, acting as a catalyst, there are the natural tensions that exist between a male and a female, simply because they are male and female.

A man who sees a girl with pretty pert breasts and a

neat round bottom in tight clothes which reveal these sexual characteristics will almost certainly feel the pull of her sexual attractiveness, even if she is his daughter. But because in our world such liaisons are regarded with horror, he may be totally unable to face up to such feelings in himself and will try to bury them; or turn them around and project them on to her ("She must be a bad 'un to make me feel like that. It can't be my fault."); or on to someone else such as his wife ("You're her mother, why do you let her get away with such behavior? What sort of a woman are you to rear a daughter like that?"); or the boy who comes courting ("You've only got to look at him to see he's a bad sort – what does he do for a living? What sort of family does he come from? He's a layabout, a drugtaker. I'm going to throw him out.").

A mother recognizing her son's sexuality in the same instinctive way will also not be able to contemplate such feelings in herself and will handle them similarly, either turning on the son or, more commonly, on any girls he brings home ("She looks a bit clever–clever to me, dear – not your type at all – you'd better watch out that she doesn't try to tie you down."); or, much more often, by trying to pull him back into babyhood, where of course he has no sexuality and all is safe between them. She encourages illness in which her son may well collude if, over the years, she has managed to make being ill in bed a more agreeable experience than being up and about his own affairs ("I don't like the sound of that cough, dear, I really don't. You stay in bed and I'll bring you an aspirin and a hot drink." "Thanks, Mom, I don't really feel very well.") or, if he won't, then she fusses over his health in a way that implies that without her constant watchfulness he will disappear into disease or even death.

The mother twittering on about coats and sweaters,

dry socks and wrapping-up-warm, dear is such a classic figure of fun that she must be based on a very widespread reality indeed; and we have no way of knowing how many girls have in fact been put off a man because a too-solicitous mother has made him appear sickly in their eyes.

Yet another way in which a mother can involve herself with an adolescent son's sexuality (and, indeed, with an adult son's come to that) is by involving him in hers. Rather than trying to make him ill she is ill in her own right, with pains based entirely on her reproductive functions, which gave him life, of course. Contemporary literature, movies and jokes are heavily larded with examples, often made more pointed by using the archetype of the sexually possessive mother, the Jewish one.

For example, in the film *Play It Again, Sam*, Woody Allen says to the girl he fancies but fears, "Of course I remembered your birthday, it's the same day as my mother had her hysterectomy."

In Philip Roth's novel, *Portnoy's Complaint*, in the middle of the sustained shriek of agony which it is, and which makes it so often so uproariously funny, the central character describes an episode when he saw his mother's menstrual blood, was horrified yet fascinated by it, and the way he was sent to the drugstore to buy her sanitary napkins. This book, perhaps more than any other, describes the effect on a boy of a seductive, possessive, manipulating, castrating mother. Exaggerated? Possibly. The character himself says that he is "living in the middle of a Jewish joke," but in fact it is not so funny, and far from restricted to one religion. Stories like Portnoy's are played out in every social group, in many different ways, over and over again.

Ian was the only son of Sheila and Harold, a Scottish

Calvinist couple who lived in London. He had been born when Sheila was thirty-five via a caesarian section. She had had three stillborn babies before him, and he was her "last chance. I swore to God, if this time I didn't have a live baby, I would just cut my throat, and finish. And he sent me you." She had told him this story many times from his earliest childhood and he had taken pleasure in it; to be so special, to be the one whose life had saved his mother's, was to be very special indeed.

He and his mother were very close, forming an alliance against Harold, his father, who was an accountant. He was a quiet man of few words and made a strong contrast to his wife, who was mercurial, rather given to dramatic gestures and self-aggrandizement, but clearly devoted to her husband and son. However, there was no doubt in Ian's mind that the family was made up of himself and his mother on one side, and his father on the other. They weren't exactly divided, but this was the way they combined.

When Ian was thirteen Sheila found him with a pornographic magazine, masturbating. She had walked into his bedroom without knocking – he was supposed to be there doing his homework – and when she saw what was happening she began to scream. She dragged the magazine from him and threw it out of the window, still screaming. Harold had come running (it was a Sunday afternoon) and was just in time to see Sheila faint, somewhat spectacularly.

The guilt which filled Ian was colossal, and he labored under it for what seemed like weeks but was probably little more than a few days. (The information for this history was given many years later, from memory, not from a written record.) Then one afternoon when he came home from school Sheila said she wanted to talk to him. She wanted him to know, she

194 RELATED TO SEX

said, why she had been so upset at what had happened. It was because she wanted him to have a healthy attitude toward sex, a pure one rather than a disgusting one; a boy who used that sort of magazine could get into the wrong sort of behavior. Hadn't the magazine itself led him into the behavior she'd seen? She was sure that once he realized that his body was a special gift, to be treated with reverence and not to be abused like that, he'd be a happier boy. She went on to tell him that she had suffered dreadfully to give him birth, and that was why she loved him so much. *And she began to unbutton her dress.*

Ian, speaking years later, said, "I felt sick. Even now, remembering it, I feel cold. I watched her undoing her buttons and I couldn't move. She was bare in the middle. I mean, she was wearing white pants and a bra, but her middle skin was bare. I still couldn't move, and she pulled down the front of her pants and showed me her belly and it was dreadful, a great puckered scar with the skin of her belly sort of hanging down on each side, like the way cloth looks when there's a tight seam in the middle of it. 'That's what I did for you,' she said. 'That's what I suffered for you,' and I began to cry. Thirteen years old and I began to cry and couldn't stop. I finished up being sick and she held my head and then put me to bed with a hot water bottle and made me hot milk and I was sick again, and she was marvelous. After that we were even closer, but I felt different." He couldn't explain in what way he felt different. (He was talking now to a marriage guidance counselor.)

Later Sheila told him about sex more specifically, with a lot of emphasis on the mechanical aspects of reproduction, especially from the female point of view. "It was like a lesson in gynecology," he said. He was then sixteen.

When he was eighteen his father took him on one

side to discuss sex with him, obviously embarrassed and under great stress, and said that his mother had asked him to talk to Ian. The question was – and it took much circumlocution to get it out – was Ian homosexual? Because if he was, they would get him to doctors, there was no need to be afraid, they'd do anything to get the right treatment for him and make him well.

Ian, by this time attending university and not as naïve as he had once been, was first amused and then infuriated. Amused at their view of homosexuality as some sort of disease (he was studying sociology and knew better!) and infuriated because they had dared to make such an accusation (which suggests that Ian himself was somewhat ambivalent in his view of the "normality" of homosexuality). The fact that he didn't bring girls home or tell his parents of his girlfriends did not mean he had none, he told his father. He did, but he kept them away because he didn't want to upset his mother.

This conversation resulted in another scene with Sheila, who said he was wicked to think his girlfriends would upset her – or was there something wrong with these girls he was consorting with that he was ashamed to bring them home? He assured her there was not and agreed to bring them home. In fact, at that time there was no special friend, but a few different ones, and Ian had no sexual contact with any of them, and was instead masturbating regularly. But even so, each of the girls he brought seemed, when he saw them at home, even less approachable, and gradually he dropped them all.

"I now realize," he told the counselor, "that she was saying and doing all sorts of subtle things to put them down, but I didn't realize it *then*."

Then, at almost twenty-one, he met a girl at college

in his last year. Christine was a somewhat masterful lady who swept him into marriage so fast he hardly knew what had happened, he said. He loved her dearly and they could have been happy, but despite many advantages – such as the fact that she had her own apartment, so that they had a home to start married life in, and that he got a good job almost immediately after graduation – they still had problems.

He was unable to consummate the marriage; he could only reach orgasm by masturbation, which Christine was willing to do for him – but he could not bring himself to help her to orgasm in the same way, which meant she had to do it for herself. This she could not cope with, and it was this that eventually brought them to marriage guidance.

The couple needed over a year of combined psychotherapy and Masters-and-Johnson-type sex therapy to resolve their difficulty, which in fact they eventually did. However, the relationship between Ian and his parents broke down completely, because he realized that he would not be able to cope with married life unless he rejected them. Not an ideal solution, both he and his counselor agreed, but he felt it was better than losing his marriage. At the time of writing, Ian and Christine have a two-year-old son, and she is pregnant again. Ian feels that soon he may be able to reestablish contact with his parents. If they will accept him, that is.

Emotional blackmail of one kind or another is a commonplace transaction in any relationship. "You do this for me, and I'll do that for you," is one form, and a fairly direct one. "Look how I suffered for you," which was the type Sheila used, is more a devious one, and more difficult to resist. In the "If you'll do this, I'll do that" dialogue, at least there is an element of choice; in the "look how I have suffered" one there is none at all.

Even more difficult to resist is projection. If a person who cannot cope with his or her own feelings turns them around and behaves as though the feelings are coming from someone else, or, alternatively, as though another person is displaying the behavior that calls forth the feelings so that no blame can be attached to the person who has them, then the object of that projection can be caught in a trap from which there seems no escape, and collusion with the projector becomes inevitable. In this way are self-fulfilling prophecies made.

For example, the man who feels an intense sexual jealousy of his new son may say, "He'll never come to anything. He'll never be anything but trouble. I have a premonition," and then makes sure over the ensuing years that the boy is treated in such a way that he will inevitably fulfill the prophecy. We all respond to the emotional stimuli we are given in a fairly straight-forward way. Expect good behavior and obedience from a child, and it's very likely you'll get it; assume that the child will misbehave the minute authority turns its back and the child will do just that. It isn't cussedness in a child. It's a natural human response.

Tragically, it can ruin some families.

Dear Claire,

What can I do? I'm fifteen, and I'm so unhappy. Me and my dad used to be very close, he said I was so sensible and all that and it was really nice having someone I could always talk to about my schoolwork, because my mom was never that interested. But in the last year he's got really moody. He won't let me go out with my friends and he goes mad if I say I want to go to a party or anything and I've got to come in at night at 10 P.M. and anyway I'm only allowed out two nights a week. My mom tried to get him to listen to her, she says it's natural for a girl to want to go out, but as I said, he goes mad. He says I can't have boyfriends till I'm twenty-one, and when my mom said to him that it's eighteen nowadays when people get the key to the door, he said: "In my house it's twenty-one, and that's the way it is." Then he said, "And if I don't like the boys she brings home then she won't be allowed out with them however old she is." I've got a boyfriend at school and I have to meet him secretly and I love him very much, but I don't dare bring him home. Once a few weeks ago Dad hit me because he said he'd seen me in town with a boy, but it wasn't me at all, and then when I swore on his life it wasn't, he got even madder and hit me again. I can't stand it much more. He said after the last fight that he was only trying to protect me, that fellas these days are bad and they'll get me pregnant and then dump me, and he knows because he used to be a young fella himself, and then he's all nice again for a while until I ask again to go out. I want to know – can I leave home now? I can't stand this much longer and my boyfriend says his mom will let me move in with them. The thing is, I'm really scared. Will my dad send the police after me?

Dear Claire,

My father is making life rather difficult for me, and I'm beginning to get very nervous and depressed. The trouble is my sister got pregnant when she was seventeen and had to go away and have the baby adopted. She's married now, and she says the only reason they are married is because she took the first boy who came along just to get away from our father. He really is so strict that he makes life hell. He won't let me wear makeup though I'm sixteen now and all my friends do, and he raises all sorts of arguments about why I can't go out, though he doesn't mind me having my girl friends at home. He'd go mad if I brought back boys, I think, so I never do. I'm determined not to end up like my sister, with an unhappy marriage and still miserable about the baby she had to give up, but I can see how it happened to her, with my father being like he is. What can I do? Don't tell me to talk to my mother. She knows how it is, but she says nothing, and I suppose she can't, because he's her husband and she has to live with him, I suppose, long after we're grown up.

Tensions across the sexes are perhaps easier to understand than some of those that occur within the sexes – from mother to daughter or from father to son. But they can be just as painful for the participants.

Dear Claire,
    My daughter is making life very unhappy for all the family. Ever since she started her periods she's been impossible. I put it down at first to hormone problems and took her to the doctor, but she gets worse and worse. She won't do as she's told, she is cheeky to me and to her father, though he takes her side all the time and says I'm on her back too much. But any mother would be. She's barely seventeen but she plasters her face with makeup and wears the most disgusting clothes until she looks like a real tart, and so I've told her, because I believe in speaking my mind. What sort of mother would I be if I didn't object to her going around looking like some painted madam? And the sort of people she makes friends with are awful. I'm not a snob, but some of them would honestly make you feel sick just to look at, let alone to talk to. These boys with greasy hair halfway down their backs and swearing like troopers. I'm not used to such things, and so I've told her.

It is painful to be the mother of an adolescent girl. The change from childhood to adulthood is slow; breasts and hips don't develop overnight. Because it is slow many mothers are able to ignore it at first, to pretend it isn't happening, to see their daughters still as straight-up-and-down little girls. But one day the truth has to impinge. It may be on the first day of the summer holidays, seeing her in her swimsuit. Did she have that bust last year? Did men look at her that way last year? *Did my own age show so much last year?*

This, of course, is the source of much of the pain. You look at that smooth, young skin, those firm breasts and that flat belly, and think of your own slowly wrinkling face and the stretch marks that lie glistening white across your own belly and the way your breasts are softer and dangle more now than they did, and you look again at the arrogantly young and perfect creature whose birth left some of these very marks on your body, and you feel the jealous anger rise. "It's not fair."

I know. I've felt it.

And it's no sin to feel it. It isn't unnatural or unloving or wicked, any more than it is wicked or unnatural for a man to feel the same about his son's young manhood and feel the rage of the threatened "king of the jungle" faced with a rival for supremacy. The only thing that can be said to be wrong is denial of those feelings, refusal to accept them as wryly as you accept other happenings in your life, with humor as well as regret. The wicked thing is to allow such buried feelings to explode into cruel treatment of the young adults you yourself created. They have committed no sin in growing up. But you will, if you make it more difficult for them than it needs to be.

12
Problems...

WHEN DOES THE NORMAL become abnormal? When does health become disease? When does right become wrong?

Impossible philosophical questions, these, because there are so many variables: there can never be an absolute morality. What is normal, healthy and right in one place at one time becomes the reverse later on in another. In biblical times in the Middle East it was normal, healthy and right for a man to have a great many wives and concubines and for adulteresses to be stoned to death. In Britain and the United States today such behavior is unthinkable.

So is it with family relationships. Each one is a continuum with, at one end, happiness and social acceptance of behavior and attitudes, and at the other misery and behavior that is shunned and spat upon by other people. It is impossible to define the middle line that separates them.

So far in this book I have tried to concentrate on the "normal" end of the continuum; looking at the way people respond to the tensions of family life created by and involving sexual and gender feelings. I have tried to show how common – and therefore, by definition, how normal – they are. Here and there I have slipped across the middle line into the problem area, precisely because it is so difficult to see where the line falls. In the next two chapters I will concentrate on the other end of the continuum where problems lie, but here again the likelihood is that I will occasionally slip across the line back to the "normal" end – and for the same reason. That line is impossible to see.

What sort of problems can sexual tensions create in a family? The one that springs immediately to mind is, of course, incese, the Big Taboo. This has already been touched upon in chapter 10 in considering the relationships between brothers and sisters. But for most people the aspect of the word that brings up the biggest frisson of horror is the idea of father/daughter incest.

Attitudes to this are extremely interesting. As an advice columnist, I receive about 40,000 letters every year. Of those, a large number seek help with sexual problems, and frequently women who write letters describing vaginismus or frigidity (an inaccurate but well-understood word describing a woman's inability to respond to sexual activity with adequate pleasure) will, quite unprompted, refer their difficulties back to sexual molestation by their father, or sometimes by their brother, and sometimes by an uncle.

When I once published such a letter on my page (they don't often appear there, even though they are well represented in the mail bag because, frankly, the newspaper's editors are as upset by the mere idea as anyone else) I said in my answer that the girl was not unique because this sort of experience with a father "happens to thousands of girls every year."

As a result of that publication I received even more letters from girls and women who had experienced sexual approaches from their fathers, many showing gratitude for the comfort they found in knowing they were not alone, and even more seeking personal sexual help. But, in addition, I had letters from psychiatrists asking me on what evidence I had based the statement that it "happens to thousands of girls every year," pointing out Freud's finding that many of his patients who talked of sex with their fathers were displaying fantasy, and Jung's opinion that these fantasies display the human capacity for creative imagination, since in one sense incestuous fantasy is concerned with the ideal rather than with actuality.

I was able to answer that question from my own experience of letters seeking help; some 2,000–2,500 letters each year refer to such experiences, and not in a way that I would associate with fantasy. Fantasy letters, of course, do arrive on advice columnists' desks, but they are usually immediately recognizable. Long, carefully written accounts of sexual experiences, couched in fancy language but with no hint of any real emotional feeling, are suspect; so are letters which pulsate with romantic imagery of the type made familiar by romance magazines ("My heart beat like a drum"; "His eyes gleamed with tears"; etc.). Letters mentioning father/daughter incest are rarely like that. They do not go into salacious detail, but veer away from the subject as soon as it is actually mentioned. Also, there is guilt, shame, self-accusation and many indications of a dependent personality – all of which are known by experienced clinicians to be typical of such daughters.

How can I tell from just one letter that the writer is dependent, passive, guilty? It shows clearly, over and over again, in so many little details. This letter is typical of hundreds.

Dear Claire,

I read that letter in your column from the girl who had problems with her lovemaking with her husband because of what her father did, and I was glad to read it because the same happened to me, when I was seventeen, nine years ago. I've always felt so bad about it, I can't look people in the face. I don't know if I can do anything about my marriage now, because like the lady that wrote, whenever my husband touches me I just see my father's face and it's dreadful how bad that makes me feel, and I can't do what he wants in bed. He gets very angry and says I don't try but I do, but how can I tell him why I feel like this? He'd go after my father and he's a big man, my husband, and he'd hurt him and that would be bad because it would be my fault, and I do worry about it. Can you please tell me what to do? I'll do whatever you say, because I want to make things better for my husband so that we can all be happy. We have three children and I want them to grow up better than I did, but I don't know how to make it right for them, with no one to tell me, and my husband doesn't talk much really, about the children, he says they are all right and I'm the one that's difficult, but I do try not to be.

And so on and on, for two more pages of apologies, self-abasement and helplessness. It doesn't need much more, I would have thought, to display a dependent passive personality. Prolonged psychotherapy in a clinical situation might confirm it, but that is all.

Buried aggression surfacing as passivity? Very possible—but it is the surface that matters in this situation. And all the evidence that is available suggests that incest is more likely where the daughter displays passive dependent personality traits.

What evidence is there apart from one advice columnist's experience? Remarkably little that can be regarded as satisfactory, possibly because of the taboo. Only a few cases actually reach the courts, and marginally more reach a doctor's or therapist's office. Various surveys have put the incidence at from 1–2 cases per million people in the United States (see Weinberg, S. K., *Incest Behavior*, Citadel Press, 1955); 1–9 per million in Europe (Master, R., *Patterns of Incest*, Psycho Sexual Study, Julian Press, 1963); to as high as 4 percent among unselected psychiatric patients in County Antrim, Ireland (Lukianowicz, N., *British Journal of Psychiatry*, 1972); and the startling figures published in *MS* in 1977: "One girl out of every four in America will be sexually abused before she reaches the age of eighteen . . . In a survey made by the American Humane Association it was found that 34 percent of such molestations take place in her [the victim's] own home," the context carrying the clear implication that most of these abusers were fathers.

The overall feeling among most psychiatrists, sociologists *et al* is that the more sober figures in fact represent only the tiny tip of the iceberg, and that the sort of figures quoted in *MS*, if not as scientifically valid as those produced by careful surveys, are more likely to be right.

Possibly the reason there is considerable confusion over the facts, as well as over attitudes, is the way incest taboo anger is mixed with child-sex taboo anger. The idea of adults using pre-pubertal children for their own sexual gratification is one that arouses extreme repugnance in a large number of people. At the time of writing there is a great deal of uproar about the publication of pornographic material using child models, and an attempt is being made to pass new protective legislation.

But there can be small doubt that there are many adults who find the idea of sex with a pure, innocent and above all immature child very seductive. Films like *Taxi Driver*, in which Jodi Foster plays a child prostitute, pandered to such tastes. So does the more recent *Pretty Baby*, with twelve-year-old Brooke Taylor in a similar role. At the much lower level – definitely sub-liminal, in fact – the film *Bugsy Malone*, in which children played the parts of adult gangsters and prosti-tutes in a pastiche of a Twenties "gangland" movie (the sort that used to star George Raft or James Cagney), titillated the same tastes.

But incest does not always involve *children*. We are back in murky semantic waters here; the word "children" can be used to describe very mature adults indeed. A man who has sex with his child may in fact have been seduced by his twenty-year-old daughter. (Remember the film *Chinatown*? The father, played by John Huston, ostensibly seduced his daughter, played by Faye Dunaway, but she was very seductive, very provocative, in her behavior. Who was seduced by whom?) He is a very different case from the man who forcibly uses his eleven-year-old girl against her will, or without her understanding. Yet over and over again people think something like "Incest – that's people having sex with their own children – that means child abuse – dreadful, dreadful, dreadful."

So at this point it is necessary to try to untangle some of these confused attitudes.

Incest between father and daughter does not always involve coercion of an immature innocent child. An adolescent girl may be well aware of her sexual attrac-tions and quite deliberately set out to captivate her own father, who is, after all, the man she knows best and often can trust the most. A boy of her own age may seem far less attractive to her simply because he is her own age, and because he may, if she becomes sexually involved with him, threaten the integrity of her home life. The girl may fear that sex outside the family circle will distress her father, who loves her – yet she wants sex. So, she seeks it from her father. He, in his turn, deeply emotionally involved with this child of his (for if he were not, she would not fear the effects on him of having sex with an outsider), is very vulnerable to her provocation.

Or there may be persuasion from another (and to some people, surprising) source. It is not unusual in cases of incest for the mother not merely to collude in what is going on, but to actively promote it. A woman whose own libido has dwindled away and who finds her husband's sexual demands tedious may turn to her almost grown daughter for help in much the same way she would seek her help with housework or the care of younger children. In the past, in remote rural communities where there was little opportunity for a horny man to get sexual satisfaction outside the family circle, the use of the nearest and most accessible female would make sense to all concerned. So, mother would either overtly or covertly lead her daughter to her own marriage bed, and sleep sounder herself at night as a result. And often the family would live in closer harmony as another result.

It was not only in the past that this happened. In Ireland recently a girl served a prison sentence for murdering her incestuous father. Her mother colluded in the father's (often violent) incest, referring to her daughter as her father's "fancy bit."

Further evidence for this? It comes from many sources. Country doctors and parsons often know of such cases and are uneasy but powerless to do much about them. It can also be a matter of common local knowledge; rare was the rural community where, in the early years of this century, there was not a family or two that "respectable" villagers kept away from or regarded with a slightly scornful tolerance because they "didn't behave right." And the fact that such families often included retarded members added to the evidence. *Not* because inbreeding always produces half-wits, but because low intelligence means a low morality threshhold (the slow-witted have more difficulty identifying what their brighter neighbors regard as the obvious difference between right and wrong), and these people would therefore become involved in incest more easily. Also, the slow-witted don't dissimulate as well as the more intelligent – and the neighbors would be more likely to know what was going on.

For further evidence I turn again to my own mailbag, but I can also report that my experience is shared by colleagues on other newspapers and magazines. Those letters which describe cases of incest do not always seek help with sexual problems. Quite a number of them come from girls who find themselves trapped in a sexual situation they no longer want. The girl who "seduced" her father at a time when the relationship with him was what she wanted and needed may later be ready to move on, but not know how to do so.

Dear Claire,

When I was twelve my mom and dad broke up for a year, because they couldn't get on, and it was a very bad time. Then my dad came back and they settled down again, and I was very happy. When I was fourteen, my mom was very ill and had to go to the hospital and I know it shouldn't have happened, but in trying to help my dad feel better about being on his own with me we got sexual. You know what I mean. Then my mom got better and came home but me and my dad were the same as when mom was in hospital, as she still wasn't all that well. She's still a bit ill and can't do much though she's better than she was. Now I have met a boy who is eighteen, a year older than me, and I want to go out with him but I don't know what to do. I don't want to upset my dad or my mom, because they are so happy, and I still remember how bad it was when he went away for a year when I was twelve. But how can I stop my dad being sexual with me now? It would make him really upset if I did but I know it is wrong to do what we do so I can't say anything or my dad will get into trouble with the police. And suppose I was to get pregnant, what would my boyfriend think? I lie awake and think and think about what to do and I get so mixed up. I feel like a bad flower that's growing in the middle of the fields.

If there was any coercion in this situation it is hard to detect it, or from which side it came. Two people seeking comfort at a time when they were filled with the fear of loss of a person beloved by both of them – it hardly sounds like the sort of scene of depravity conjured up by the word "incest." Nor could it have been so painful for either father or daughter, since the sexual relationship went on quietly for the next three years. But what happens when the daughter is ready for a new relationship, and wants to get involved with a boy of her own age? She has so far enjoyed the situation she is in, and anyway doesn't want to cause distress to the people she loves. And over all hangs the threat of discovery and the fuss that would be made. No wonder she feels like "a bad flower" which is as elegant a description of the emotional effects of ambivalence as any I've ever read. And the letter was full of misspellings and so badly written as to be almost illegible; far from the outpourings of a sophisticated, educated mind.

One of the most difficult things to cope with for most people who have never thought much about incest is the idea that it is, in a sense, perfectly *normal*. That is, there is no relation between incest and the so-called "perversions" – incestuous fathers are no more likely to be interested in bestiality, sadomasochism or exhibitionism or any other -ism than other fathers. This is not to say that an incestuous father is never a sadist or whatever as well; it can happen. But it is incidental, not inevitable.

The only thing that can be said for sure about a man who gets into an incestuous relationship with his daughter is that he has not been held back by the same taboo that controls the rest of us. This does not mean that he is less "moral" or less strong, simply that the control slipped. It could slip because of factors such as poverty, anxiety or low intelligence; and it is true that there is a somewhat higher incidence of incest among families which are poor, underprivileged or low in IQ. *But by no means all such cases are confined to such people.*

This is one of the comforting falsehoods behind which educated, middle class people have hidden for years, which makes it much more painful for them when in fact their own control slips and they find themselves sexually involved with a pubescent daughter.

The following cases were collected from a psychiatrist specializing in criminology, often called as an expert witness in trials. They cover a period of some ten years.

John K. Engineer. Married eleven years when his wife died. Three children – a girl aged ten and boys aged eight and four at the time of their mother's death. When the girl was seventeen, as a result of a report by a next-door neighbor who had observed the activity in their house through an adjacent bedroom window, he was charged with incest with his daughter. He committed suicide by gassing himself while on bail. The boys had been put into an institution and remained there until each reached the age of eighteen. The older one joined the army and seemed settled. The younger became uncontrollable, was often in trouble with the police and was killed in a road accident at the age of nineteen. The sister, who had been sent to live with her maternal aunt, committed suicide, also using gas, the day after her brother's death.

Psychiatrist's comment: It was the exposure and the bringing to trial which broke up this family, not the actual incest. At the time I saw this man and the children, allowing for the inevitable distress because of the situation they were in, they were adjusted and content. It seems unlikely that the girl would have died when she did had the family not been broken by the father's suicide. It is tempting to surmise that with an adequate home life the young boy would not have become the petty criminal he did, and possibly also would have escaped his accidental death. But that is mere surmise.

Gordon J. Bricklayer. Served three years for incest after daughter, aged seventeen, laid a complaint at the local police station at the instigation of her mother. While he was in prison his daughter lived with her mother and seven younger brothers and sisters and then, when he was due for discharge, applied for a job as a resident hospital orderly. Her father, when he arrived home from prison, became drunk and beat his wife; he was warned by the police, who were called by neighbors, that he would be in court again if he "didn't watch it." He said he didn't care – he'd "swing" for what they'd done to him. The police judged it safe to leave him after some talking and left. Gordon then attacked his wife again, after which she gave him their daughter's new address (this was explained by one of the other children, afterwards). Gordon then went to the hospital, found the girl's room (he said he was her father, so he was allowed to go into the residence) and attacked her with a knife. He is now serving a long sentence for serious assault.

Psychiatrist's comment: This man's total inability to see that he was in any way involved in his own actions – he remains convinced that he was first enticed by his daughter and then "informed on" by his wife – has converted his initial family problem into a major criminal offence. It is hard to say whether his claim and resulting rage are justified; certainly the mother is a very manipulative woman, and the daughter particularly docile. I can never get a word out of her, even when I am able to separate her from her mother. What will happen when Gordon leaves prison in a few years' time I cannot say, of course, but I would not be surprised if he attacked the mother and daughter again, or even murdered one or both. He feels extremely aggrieved.

Peter S. Chemist. Three times attempted suicide with tablets and on the fourth tried to drive his car into a tree. Taken to court on a charge of dangerous driving, and referred for a psychiatric opinion. Admitted to a mental hospital, where, after some time, he admitted to deep anxiety about sexual feelings for his daughter, a married woman of twenty-three. He denied any sexual contact with her with great vehemence; however, his daughter, invited to talk to the psychiatrist, said there had been several episodes when she was eleven which had ended when she had her first period. She felt no apparent distress over this; he had been gentle and she had enjoyed the experience, she said. Her own marriage was happy and sexually successful. Peter's depression had dated from this time in her childhood, she agreed. Her mother had known nothing of it, and never would, she assured the psychiatrist, "because I've got enough to worry about, being their only child." Peter, when told what his daughter had said, became very distressed and withdrew even further into depression. He is still in the hospital and, despite periods when he seems rather better following electric shock treatments, he relapses frequently.

Psychiatrist's Comment: This is what could be called a case of terminal depression. I have no doubt that eventually he will succeed in committing suicide. His guilt and anger about this episode with his daughter are irreconcilable with his continuing desire for her. He's a very sick, unhappy man. I'm very sorry for him.

Bill J. Laborer. His eight-year-old daughter disappeared and a police search was begun. She was eventually found dead in a closet in an empty house near her own home. She had been strangled and sexually molested. After a police investigation lasting several days, Bill was arrested and charged with her murder, and sentenced to life imprisonment. While in prison he developed a florid mental illness, becoming violent to the point of needing chemical and physical restraint. Psychotherapy was then instituted, and he confessed to a conviction that he was changing sex. However, he also showed signs of a strong sexual drive, attempting to attack wardens and other prisoners, and he was put on estrogen (apparently to damp down his testosterone levels) and tranquilizers. The psychiatrist in the prison hospital then left the service, and there was a delay before a new one arrived. The patients were looked after by a series of temporary psychiatrists in the meantime. Bill's estrogen therapy was maintained during this period, but he had no psychotherapy, remaining in the prison. He seemed better, less aggressive and more content, and, as can happen in such institutions, he was left alone as long as he caused no trouble. A new psychiatrist then arrived who examined Bill, discovered that he had developed definite breasts and other feminine characteristics, and immediately stopped the estrogen. Bill became depressed and violent again, and required restraint. In spite of this, he managed to obtain a length of heavy twine and hanged himself in his prison cell.

Psychiatrist's Comment: I was only consulted on this case after the patient's death, but from the copious notes on him, it seems to me that the "I-am-a-woman" delusion arose from his inability to face up to the fact that he had molested and killed his daughter. When his delusion was underpinned by dosages of estrogen large enough both to control his sexual urges – which estrogen in such a case would do – and also to grow breasts, he was content. A woman with a low sex drive could not rape and kill a child, ergo, he was not guilty. When the dosage was stopped abruptly and he had inadequate support and understanding of his situation, suicide was inevitable. It is interesting that a determined would-be suicide can usually attain his object, even while under surveillance in a high-security prison.

Most people considering a case like Bill's would feel a total inability to enter into his situation. To rape and kill a daughter and then go through such mental contortions – how can this be regarded as one end of a continuum that stretches back to ordinary family relationships of the sort you and I have? But look again at John's story, and imagine yourself in his lonely, unhappy situation. Is that so abnormal as to be incomprehensible? Most honest people with a spark of compassion should be able to understand and say, "Yes, given the situation that could, possibly, be me."

Those who find this attitude too "permissive" may be comforted to know that it is shared by many with direct working experience of dealing with cases of incest. A family doctor in Essex, in eastern England, who is also a magistrate, wrote as follows in the English medical journal *Pulse* in April 1977:

> To my mind the Sexual Offences Act gives adequate protection for girls under the age of thirteen, anyone having intercourse with her being liable to life imprisonment, and if the girl is over thirteen but under sixteen the maximum penalty is two years. In addition the mentally subnormal of any age is protected, and at any age if intercourse takes place without consent it amounts to rape, again punishable by imprisonment for life.
>
> The law relating to incest thus only provides additional protection for the consenting female of normal intelligence, over the age of sixteen, and one has to consider whether this advantage outweighs the disadvantages.
>
> What are these disadvantages? The greatest is that an innocent man may be convicted, generally because he pleads guilty to prevent the necessity of his daughter giving evidence at his trial. This is an important aspect because Professor Trevor Gibben's study of the child victims of sexual offences showed quite clearly that the emotional disturbance was much higher among those children who were called to give evidence in court.
>
> I am not alleging that there are many cases in which an innocent man pleads guilty, but I do say that if a law produces this result, it should at least be questioned.

There is another much larger group of those imprisoned for incest who find themselves inside because they have been "shopped" [informed on] by wives who deliberately encouraged the offence in order to land their unwanted husbands in prison. There are also those who were subjected to blackmail by their daughters, often when attention had been diverted from them to a younger sister.

In view of all these circumstances I believe that the removal of incest from the statute book would be a desirable reform. . . .

A British Medical Association (BMA) spokesman is reported to have said, "Genetic research shows nearly 50 percent of severe or moderate mental retardation among the offspring of first-degree relatives." What nonsense! I submit that it is quite impossible to substantiate this claim, for no one knows how many children are born as a result of such union.

It may well be that this figure is correct for the progeny of *known* incestuous relationships, but this is largely because the facts are more likely to become known in the case of those of sub-normal intelligence, whereas the more intelligent offender in all probability will escape detection. Surely the truth of the matter is that any heredi-tary characteristics will be accentuated in the case of a child born as a result of a first-degree union, a fact that is clearly demonstrated by inbreeding among animals.

Where both partners are highly gifted it is likely that their children will be also; where both are of low intelligence the progeny may well be of even less ability. . . .

I do not say that incest is a good thing: as the

father of three daughters I can say that I have never felt the least desire to indulge in such a practice.

What I do say is that any possible advantages which the law may have in protecting certain women are more than neutralized by the possible abuses to which it can be put. . . .

So far, we have considered only father/daughter incest and brother/sister incest. But there is another form, one that seems to create a particular frisson of its own – not so much of horror as distaste or guffaws.

The idea of a woman having sex with her son is one many people simply cannot encompass. Father / daughter incest is just about imaginable for most of us – but what sort of man is it who would find a woman twice his age sexually attractive?

The worldwide hooha recently made over the private life of Britain's Princess Margaret was based much more on the fact that the man she chose as her friend after her marriage breakdown was sixteen years her junior, than on the fact that she, like many millions of others throughout the world, was flouting her marriage vows. The cynical gossips implied that he was only interested in her money, her power, her prestige.

Yet when contemplating a relationship in which the man is much older than his new wife or mistress, most people are quite approving. The man is admired as a success – for only a successful man could attract a smooth-cheeked, luscious young bride – and she is regarded as fortunate indeed in having ensnared so mature, wise and sexually experienced a partner. It is rarely assumed that the couple do not genuinely love each other.

But when an older woman and a younger man pair up the giggles and sneers come from all over – and the general assumption is that he must have an ulterior motive, because he couldn't possibly care for her, not *really* care.

A similar reaction greets the idea of mother/son incest. At most it gets a giggle: "Oedipus, shmoedipus, so long as he loves his mother."

Perhaps one reason for this is the fact that Freud dwelt so heavily on the Oedipus myth in his work, and ascribed so many problems to oedipal conflict. He made such relationships seem commonplace and therefore rather funny.

Yet it isn't funny, any more than father/daughter incest is, and it can obviously create as many problems within a family, as many complex strands. Yet, interestingly, throughout my own research into family relationships, in all the letters I have received on the subject, I can remember very few indeed – if any – on genuine mother/son incest.

I have had letters from women describing such episodes, but in such flowery language, and in such pornographic detail, that it has clearly been a fantasy. I have had similar letters from men, often describing scenes in which the mother started to beat the boy with a strap for some misdemeanor, and which turned into frank sexual activity when the youngster lost his temper and began to beat her back. These, too, read like extracts from an underground Victorian book, and they shriek "fantasy" in every sentence.

None of the psychiatrists to whom I have talked over the years have been able to tell of mother/son incest cases, and few such cases seem to reach the courts. Yet, obviously, they happen, for undertones of oedipal feelings appear in many books, plays and popular songs. *Hamlet; Portnoy's Complaint;* "I want a girl just like the girl who married dear old Dad"; D. H. Lawrence's *Sons and Lovers*, and so on. And what appears in popular entertainment is always a reflection of what is going on in people's minds, whether they realize it or not.

13

...And More Problems

IDENTIFYING WITH AN incestuous rapist is difficult, but identifying with the needs of a transvestite is less so. Most "normal" men would feel absurd dressed up as women, but are unlikely to feel horrified at the idea. After all, drag shows of one kind or another have been staple fare for the entertainment industry for many years, ranging from the outrageous Dame of classical English pantomime via semiamateur "cabarets" in bars to the elegant sophistication of female impersonators in the glossiest of revues. In the United States almost every major city has its drag theater, drag bars and drag clubs, and in Germany and Holland men in false eyelashes have been part of the scene since before the 1930s. All this follows centuries of transvestite performing, including the Commedia D'el Arte, Shakespeare's Globe players, Morris dancers, morality plays and African tribal displays.

The whole question of what is normal in dress is really an absurd one. Clothes themselves are basically absurd. They have a function – to protect us from the climate – but for most of us this functional importance comes far below their display value.

Fashion has decreed over the centuries that men's display should vary from the wildly gorgeous, worn with face paint and exotically curled wigs, to the starkly puritanical and back again. Even in our own

era we have watched men move from drab between-
the-wars' conservatism via the nostalgic peacockery of
the "Edwardian" of the post war years to the bearded,
flower-bedecked comfort of a decade later. Then came
unisex and the ubiquitous blue jean began its reign,
which still goes on.

Side by side with all this has gone a bewildering rate
of change in women's clothes, as style moved from
"pretty-pretty" to "oh-my-God-bizarre," skirts whizzed
up and down with frenetic indecision, and faces were
painted every color of the rainbow and a few more
besides.

So who can say what is normal feminine dress and
what is normal male dress? Apparently transvestites
can.

It's only when I'm wearing my women's clothes
that I feel "right," you know? Every day I walk
out of here in my neat dark suit with my white
shirt and sober tie and go to the office, and every
evening I ache to get back here and be comfortable
in silk underwear, with my legs smooth and satiny
in tights, and frilled petticoats under my full skirt.
I spend a lot of money on my clothes – dresses,
underwear, jewelry, the whole lot. Wigs too, of
course. I never wear hats – I don't know many like
me who do – but wigs, long curled ones, or smooth
sleek ones, lots of those. I'm not gay, you know.
None of my friends like me are, either. We meet at
a special club for TVs, I read about in one of those
fringe magazines – we're all much the same. Got
wives, you know, and kids. Two of the men are very
lucky. Their wives understand, even let them make
love when they're dressed, which is my dearest
ambition – but mine couldn't cope, I don't think.

She's competitive, you see. She'd think I was getting at her. But I wouldn't be, I just love to wear my special clothes and feel good. Happy, serene inside, that's the way I feel. I don't know what'll happen when my wife finds out. She will, of course, one day. You see, she thinks I'm writing a book, and that's why I shut myself up in my study every night and wont let anyone come in. Well, I am, in fact. I'm writing about what it's like to be me, and about the way I want to go out in the street in my clothes. One day she'll say, "Isn't that book finished yet?" and then I suppose I'll have to do something. Tell her, maybe, but I don't know how.

When I talked to this man at his home one weekend in 1976 when his wife had taken their two children to visit her parents, he was wearing a curled wig of the Rita Hayworth type, heavy makeup through which his rather heavy beard stubble showed clearly, false eyelashes with "doe-eye" lines painted around his eyes in the style that was popular in the 1950s. His clothes too were from the same era – a full skirt, electric blue, over pale blue multifrilled petticoats, a lacy white blouse with a great many chains and beads and big button earrings. His shoes had stiletto heels and peep-toes. The other clothes in his secret wardrobe (it was hidden in his study) were also curiously dated in look; there were neat little suits with tight skirts, reminiscent of smart secretaries of the period, which he wore with frilled jabot-fronted blouses and little white gloves; strapless dresses in tulle in pale, sugared almond colors; frothy nightgowns and negligees.

When I said I thought the clothes were old-fashioned, he agreed; he doesn't like modern styles. "Unfeminine," he said. "Real women wear soft, scented things, things that flutter and flow. They're the kind of clothes I like."

His family history was fairly uneventful, the way he told it. The younger son of a family of three, he had lower middle class parents (his father worked for the post office and his mother was a full time wife-and-mother and never took a job outside her home). She had been quiet, he said, warm and nice but quiet, while his father had been a reserved sort of man who communicated little with his children. The three of them (all boys) had grown up, married and settled down, with one brother going into the post office like their father, another opening his own successful garage, and he himself joining a large chemical firm as a production chaser. He had been with the firm for twelve years and was content in every way – except for his cross-dressing needs. As far as he knew neither of his brothers had any bizarre needs of any kind.

Other transvestites tell a similar story. They often report the need to express a softer feminine side of themselves, first making itself known in their very young years and continuing steadily and with increasing urgency as time went on. There is no evidence that the need diminishes in old age, and it may indeed increase.

Another personal account of transvestism which is of particular interest was written by a physiologist and appeared first in the medical journal *The Lancet* in October 1971.

My mother was of Puritan stock. Her first husband was a doctor who died only ten weeks after the marriage, which was never consummated. She married my father twelve years later. His background was in farming, schoolteaching, and the church. He was a "Harvard intellectual" who had decided to study medicine, but had stopped short and made a career for himself in physiology. My mother was the dominant partner, having much physical energy and a vigorous emotional temperament; my father was quiet, intellectual and artistic. I was the youngest of three sons, and it was early decided that, since I alone showed an interest in biology, I should become a doctor. Our family was very close-knit; we didn't have much to do with our neighbors.

For me to become a doctor was part of the family's mental structure, built in some years before. In my thirteenth year I first had transvestite fantasies. In a geography lesson I heard of the island community of Marken which kept boys in girls' dresses and long hair until they were fourteen. I can still clearly feel the excitement and envy with which I heard this.

At the age of twenty-five, I began unaccountably failing in my medical examinations. I was sent to a psychiatrist and had two years of analytical psychotherapy. One significant fantasy that emerged during this time was of a female patient, of my mother's build and age, who attempted to seduce me while I was conducting a physical examination on her. I was so anxious about the consequences of medical qualification that my analyst suggested that I forget medicine and pursue a career in physiology.

Within the context of this family milieu and neurotic breakdown, the development of my transvestism could be explained as follows: I imagined (or construed) my mother as wanting me to replace her first husband by becoming first a doctor and then her lover. In this she was threatening my self-realization by choosing my career for me and then forcing herself on me as a sexual partner and this in a partnership in which she would clearly be the demanding and dominant member. My reaction, in order to maintain integrity and to avoid this sexual relationship, was to try to escape by disguising myself as a girl. This reaction would have been reinforced by the general family attitude of despising girls. Thus by becoming a girl I would remove myself from the family and from all danger to myself. Neither of these steps ever occurred at the conscious level. I was quite unaware of my construct of the nature and designs of my mother until it emerged during the analysis.

Other things could have reinforced this escape reaction. From my seventh to fifteenth years I was sent to boys' private boarding schools, at all of which I was a misfit because of the powerfully expressed and unconventional views of my parents and older brothers. I affected to despise team sports, and I read far more advanced biology textbooks than was usual, and, unlike most boys of my social class and age, I had not been circumcised. At times, therefore, I was very unhappy. Becoming a girl would have removed me from this inimical environment, leading to self-preservation and reduction of tension.

During adolescence and until after I was married (at twenty-seven) – apart from very occasional opportunities for clandestine dressing in borrowed clothes – the state remained one of fantasy activity alone. Like many other transvestites, I had assumed that normal heterosexual activity within marriage would solve the problem. (My puritanical background and family cohesiveness had precluded premarital sexual experience.) The fantasies were partially relieved by marriage. My wife made many of her own clothes. We had many discussions about dress design, and I frequently assisted her in her dressmaking. I began to buy women's clothes for myself and to wear them as chances arose. With children in the house and an understandably uncooperative wife, the times available for dressing were, and still are, very limited. A sabbatical visit to another country gave me a chance of experiencing what it felt like to be dressed for a whole day at a time and for part of every day. It was during this period that I noted the decline in the fetishist aspect of the condition and the relief that accompanied the more-or-less continuous satisfaction of the compulsion.

One transvestite's wife says that she has no difficulty in talking to me as a woman when I am in woman's clothes since I seem to her then to be a more feminine person (despite my height and very masculine and hairy hands). Although I was not aware of it myself it seems a feminization of personality accompanies the partial feminization of appearance.

Obviously the partner of a transvestite also has problems.

My husband is a heterosexual transvestite. This fine-sounding title means two things. The first is an ability, willingness and pleasure in normal relations with the opposite sex, and secondly the desire and need at times to dress, partly or completely, in the clothes of the opposite sex. I know from experience that these two things can exist side by side more or less peaceably, depending on the wife's response to both aspects of her husband.

I have met several transvestites, or TVs as they call themselves, and some of their wives. It occurred to me that if I wrote down the views and opinions expressed by these men and women I could pass on the knowledge that any wife is one among many. Others do share the same horror and fears that go with transvestism.

I know of one engaged couple where the girl knows and goes along with her fiancé's wishes, but the wives to whom I have talked had all discovered after marriage. I think the emotional shattering that accompanied discovery needs no description. My own initial thoughts were a raging, "What does he think I am, a lesbian wanting a partner? What does he want of me, a male impersonation to complement his female role?" I now know that neither of these was the answer. My husband, and TVs generally, merely want of their partner a calm acceptance of themselves, good and bad, mixed as it is.

I believe that however hard a woman may work, whether as wife, housewife, mother and perhaps as worker, she is not normally under the same pressure in this beastly modern rat race of a world as the male. If she fails it is either in the home, and therefore very local, or at work, when she falls back on husband and home. If the husband fails, or gets sick, he knows that wife, home and family suffer as a result of his failure or sickness. I'm not belittling the wife's role, I know how vital a part she plays. My earnings are necessary and appreciated, but if I failed (which God forbid) we would manage. If my husband failed it would be immeasurably more difficult to cope. We rely on husbands for main or total financial backing, final authority, decisions, provision of home, food, clothing, light, heat, insurance and so on. Is it any wonder that they need to unwind at times and get away from the "provider" image? Others do it in more accepted ways, like gambling, drinking or "womanizing." Would one of these "accepted" images of relaxation be more pleasurable to live with? I think now that the answer is no. The general opinion is that they are more tolerant, more relaxed, happier, more home-loving, and better providers because they unwind in this particular way. Also, who are we to judge what is normal, right or proper? People are more important than the way they dress. If men are good fathers, good providers and good faithful husbands, should we condemn them and discard them for one aspect which offends, frightens or displeases? I think not.

Men are often selfish and babyish, wanting the best of both male prerogatives and suspected female advantages. My biggest complaint is of the expense involved. Oh, the money that must be wasted on this thing! When it is necessary to scrimp and scrape to make ends meet (and God knows how difficult that is sometimes) it is hard to bear the thought of money frittered away unnecessarily. *But* – is it any less expensive to drink, gamble or "womanize?" Again, I think not.

The wives I spoke to had, without exception, all been through one or more phases where their husbands had abandoned transvestism and tried, for periods varying from months to several years, to overcome the need. (I think it important to state here that the attempts to stop were all made from love of their wives and a genuine desire not to make them unhappy.) Clothes and accessories were ditched, regardless of cost, in order to remove temptation. In no case was this abandoning of any

use. Sooner or later they all succumbed and re-
verted to "dressing," even in cases where medical
and psychiatric help had been sought.

During our worst patch I decided to go to our
family doctor, who made provision for me to see a
psychiatrist. The resulting interview was not very
helpful. He was sympathetic but not very know-
ledgeable and held out no hope for a "cure" for my
husband. Transvestism is almost impossible to cure
for this reason: the men don't want to be cured.
They enjoy "dressing," it gives them a lot of
pleasure. If a cure is attempted it is important to
remember that as the mind is turned away from
transvestism it will turn to something else. Experience shows that, for one reason or another, it
often tends to turn to homosexuality. That is a
chance I personally would not like to take.

During attempts to stop we agreed that the
symptoms were almost frighteningly identical. The
glow of love and goodwill fostered by the attempt
gradually fades and is replaced by moodiness, bad
temper, irritability and restlessness, eventually
leading, if prolonged, to an actual nervous breakdown. Home life for everyone is intolerable. I frequently felt obliged to intervene between my
husband and our two small children during our
experience of this hellish phase. Eventually the
need to dress becomes so great that it can no
longer be resisted and they begin again – in secret.
Secrecy is no answer. They feel guilty and swings
of mood disrupt family harmony even more. Also,
laugh as folks might, I think that most women have
a funny sort of intuition that tells them when
something is not as it should be. We're not crazy,
and little pointers added together eventually make
for certainty. I found the deceit hard to bear. It was

irrational, as the "dressing" was done in secret in order to comply with my demand that I wanted to know nothing about it, but there – I don't think anyone has accused women of being rational beings. . . .

I have recently let my husband know that I was willing to accept things as they were and almost literally shook him rigid by agreeing to go to a TV party, what I call "jumping in at the deep end," hoping to prove that I could "swim." It worked. On the whole they were a decent crowd of people. It was not as terrible as I had feared. But the clinching argument came when my husband entered and I saw him, for the first time, fully "dressed." I curled up inside and vowed to myself that if he was going to "dress," as he obviously intended to continue doing, he would have to do it well, and would need help – from me.

So you see I have come full circle and from absolute antagonism I have arrived at the determination (through pride perhaps) that no husband of mine shall make an exhibition of himself, through a stubborn refusal on my part to accept and help him.

Women too may be transvestites, finding it more agreeable to dress in a "butch" style than the traditional skirted feminine way, but they have few problems today. Unisex clothes mean that the transvestite woman can wear what she wants, where she wants; fashion indeed aids and abets her, for women's trousers are now made with the fly front opening (or imitation of it) that men need on their trousers for functional purposes.

In the past when no woman ever wore trousers, of course it was different, and it is interesting that today

there are no stage performers who are male impersonators as Hetty King and Vesta Tilley were in the
early part of this century. They just are not needed.

Transsexuals too show a greater preponderancy of
men than women, but they are very different from
transvestites. They feel they are "trapped in the body
of the wrong sex" and may be so gripped by the delusion
that they seek and even obtain mutilating surgery,
losing penis and testicles and having a rudimentary
vagina shaped from remaining tissue. Many then take
large doses of estrogen to produce breasts and control
the growth of facial and body hair.

The illusion is rarely fully successful; the man who
developed through normal puberty will retain the male
bone structure and body shape – narrow hips, wide
shoulders – that his genes then decreed, and vocal
chords once enlarged and thickened to create a deep
voice cannot thin out again. However, voices can be
greatly changed by effort of will and training, though of
course large masculine hands and feet cannot be
shrunken.

There are many theories about why transsexualism
occurs. There are those who see it in totally Freudian
terms, relating to childhood experiences with parents:
the boy who wants sexual union with his mother sup-
presses the desire because of fear of the father, only to
find it reemerge as a desire to actually *be* the mother –
i.e., to dress like her or be like her. The same explana-
tion is given in reverse for the motivation of women
transsexuals.

Other theories are more physical. One suggests that
the developing fetus is profoundly affected by changes
in the mother's hormone levels during her pregnancy,
and that even a small imbalance in estrogen (female
hormone) and androgen (male hormone) – and both
sexes have some of each – at a significant developmental

phase can affect the fetal hypothalamus in the uterus and thus "condition" the baby to develop needs that run counter to its genetic structure in later life.

This is difficult to accept. If the hormonal influence was profound enough to create such thought disorders in later life, would it not be powerful enough to leave some physical stigmata as well? Would such people develop normal genitalia, experience a normal puberty, father children (and a great many of them do) if they had been so affected by adverse hormonal influence? Many psychiatrists find this theory of causation a difficult one to swallow, and it is interesting that it is widely held by transsexuals themselves. It is as though, because of shame about their state, they need an out-side cause to blame for it. Why it should be easier to blame a physical rather than psychological experience is hard to say. Probably because most of us, despite more than seventy-five years of post-Freudian thinking, still find it difficult to believe that the mind of an adult can be so powerfully affected by childhood experience. Yet clearly it is.

John is aged forty-two, married for twenty years with two teenage daughters, and he is currently waiting to go to Casablanca for "sex change" surgery for which he has been saving for almost the same twenty years (it is exceedingly expensive). He knows the operation is risky, that the surgeons who work in some of these dubious establishments are motivated entirely by cupidity and have little concern about their patient's total welfare, and that he may be made ill by what happens. But he is determined. His wife has accepted the facts of his situation, has divorced him and has custody of the children. He hopes, once the operation is over, to persuade her to be his friend, but this is really a fantasy on his part. She is bitterly angry and humiliated by her discovery of his needs and speaks of him with real hate. She is particularly angry because they were always short of money when the children were small, in spite of his status as a partner in the family firm, and the fact that he had been salting away money for such a purpose is enraging to her.

Asked to provide an account of his childhood that might explain his dilemma, he wrote the following.

I am the only child of my parents, both now dead. My father was quite old, forty-three when I was born, and my mother was thirty-nine. They married late because both of them had to look after their own parents until they died.

I remember as a child always feeling that there was something I wanted and couldn't have. My mother was not easy to talk to, though she was very kind, and my father was a bit frightening, though he talked to me more. But he talked most to my mother, who was not very healthy and spent a lot of time lying on a sofa in the living room, in her dressing gown. It was made of white lace and smelled of lilies of the valley. Whenever I smell them I think of her.

I first started to dress up in her clothes when I was about five and I quite enjoyed it though it wasn't really what I wanted. I knew that. Once I remember my father coming in and catching me and he looked at me with his face very straight and said, "You look awful."

I said, "But it's Mom's dress. You like it when she wears it. It's all right when she wears it."

"That's right," he said. "It's all right when she wears it. But she's a lady. You're not. Take it off," and he went away.

I thought, "I want to be a lady." I think that was

the first time I thought it. I thought a lot after that. I used to watch Dad sitting by my mother and talking softly to her and holding her hand while I sat in my chair and read my book the way they told me, and I'd watch them and think about how I wanted to be a lady as well.

And then, when I was thirteen, I had this sudden experience. I can't describe it exactly, I really can't. I was sitting in a field somewhere, I don't know why, whether it was a school thing or a picnic with friends or what it was. I was sitting in this field and looking at the sky and there were thick clouds low down, near the horizon, and I suddenly knew, like a flash of lightning. I knew that a dreadful mistake had been made. I was a woman, that was the thing. I didn't just want to be a lady – I really *was* one, or would be in time, and this was what the problem was. I felt marvelous at first, all excited and shining. And then I cried because it was all so awful, everyone knowing I was a boy.

Then when I was twenty-two I went to work for my father – he was an accountant like me – and then he said I ought to get married, so I did, but it was all wrong and I really knew it from the start, but what could I do? He said I should, so I did. It was all right, I suppose. Sex was boring but all right. I didn't bother much and nor did she, really, once she had the children. I started to save for my operation then, though. When I was first engaged.

That there may be a parental role involved in the rooting of the transvestite or transsexual need is fairly obvious. The idea has even surfaced in popular entertainment. In Bill MacNaughton's play *The Anniversary* (later filmed with Bette Davis, being her usual terrifying self) the effects on a family of a tyrannical mother were depicted. One of the sons is shown to be a transvestite who steals women's underwear from clothes lines. He needs them, it is implied, not so much to cross dress but as a fetish object (and indeed for some cross-dressers it is the fetish effect – that is, the sexual pleasure-enhancing – aspect of the clothes that matters most), and the blame for this "kink" is laid firmly at the mother's feet.

In the film *No Way To Treat A Lady*, Rod Steiger plays a murderer driven by the effects of a decidedly unhealthy relationship with his now dead mother to dress up as a woman in order to despatch one of his victims. (This film has other interesting overtones, incidentally. The other main protagonist, played by George Segal, is also mother-dominated; the love-hate sexual bases of the relationships permeate the film with considerable effect, as well as humor.)

Including the subject of homosexuality in a chapter devoted to problems will be very offensive to many homosexual people, who maintain that homosexuality is just one form of human sexuality, that it is normal, if less frequent than heterosexuality, and is certainly not a problem in the sense that incest and trans-sexualism are.

I agree with this viewpoint, seeing nothing at all surprising about this form of human loving. I would regard it as infinitely more of a personal problem not to be able to love at all, than to happen to find it easier to love members of one's own gender.

However, other people – that is, those who regard themselves as fully heterosexual, though how they can be *sure* is difficult to say – see it as a problem, and indeed some homosexual people themselves do. And the mere fact that there is need for a Gay Liberation movement makes it obvious that there are social problems associated with homosexuality.

For some years now there has been much argument about the causes of homosexuality. Much of the argument is based on the idea that homosexuality is some sort of illness; spot the causes, and you'll be able to prevent or "cure" it.

This is manifest nonsense (as well as offensive to a lot of healthy, happy homosexuals who would loathe to be "cured") when you remember that it has been with us ever since mankind stepped down from the trees to stand on two feet. Long before the start of the Christian era, the citizens of Sodom were told by the puritanical, anti-sex religious characters of the time not to do what they were enjoying doing, and the ancient Greeks and Romans happily engaged in homosexual love long before that. Indeed, the Greeks maintained it was the only true love, since heterosexual relations were so firmly rooted in the humdrum need to reproduce the species. Homosexuality has been part of the human experience in every culture ever studied. Yet we still find worried people today expressing dislike and anxiety about it. *Plus ça change, plus c'est la même chose.*

Since the question of cause has arisen, it is worth looking at some of the theories that have been floated.

First, there are the physical ones. Homosexual men, it has been suggested, are born deficient of the necessary male hormones. This allows basic female hormones to "take over" and makes them respond as they do to their own gender, and incidentally makes them limp-wristed and gives them a mincing gait.

This theory meets difficulties when one considers the situation of women homosexuals. Are they supposed to be born with an *excess* of male hormones? Any theory which has to turn itself on its head to accommodate both sexes has to be thrown out of court, surely.

In fact this one dates largely from the time when it was thought that there were very few, if any, female homosexuals. Despite the early history of Sappho on the Isle of Lesbos, there were many people who could not bring themselves to believe that such things could happen to women, and so they decided they didn't. They were helped in this erroneous thinking by the fact that it is easier for a woman to suppress her natural bent and to accommodate herself to heterosexual intercourse, and to give birth to children, than it is for a man. And for a very long time, women obligingly hid themselves behind the conventions.

Now they don't, so another theory was needed. It was found in Freudian ideas of childhood experience molding the adult individual. Some studies of homosexual people of both sexes have suggested that in a great many of their family histories there was evidence of a weak or absent father and a dominant mother.

It is true that there are some homosexual men who maintain a close and loving relationship with their strong-minded mothers, and indeed such relationships have become part of the stereotype image of the "gay man." But though this may be true for some, it is clear that it is by no means true for all.

The idea that family experience can give rise to profound changes in behavior and thinking is one that has also been floated as a cause of schizophrenia. The Ken Loach film *Family Life*, based on some of the theories of psychiatrist R. D. Laing and others, explored this. But the idea is difficult to accept, not least because there is no one single entity that can be labeled "schizophrenia." It is an umbrella term used to cover a large number of symptoms and signs ranging from severe illness, showing trancelike catatonic states, via mania and/or withdrawal, to the sort of mildly "antisocial" behavior that could be regarded as normal in an adolescent in a modern developed society.

With so many bewildering forms of "schizophrenia," how can there be one simple cause – like a family in which a parent constantly uses the "double bind method" of control? ("Of course I don't mind you going out. I can sit here and cry for you by myself.")

Similarly, when homosexual behavior ranges from the wildly outrageous campery of, for example, the leading character in Peter Nicholls' play *Privates on Parade* (he calls every man by a feminine version of his masculine name, wears drag whenever he can, makeup at all times) to the quiet little clerk who never has any sexual contact at all with either sex, but dreams about making love with a man – how can one theory cover them all?

Also, homosexual behavior is affected by the mood of the society in which an individual lives; in some theatrical circles in New York and London, being homosexual is a benefit, and admits a man to the Inner Circle. So by allowing what might usually be a hidden aspect of his personality to emerge, an actor may gain considerably. And there are plenty who pretend to be gay when they very definitely are not, for the same reason.

Taking an overall view, it seems unlikely that there is any single identifiable family cause for homosexual behavior, any more than there is any one cause for our wide range of heterosexual behavior. All we can say is that we are programed to seek and find sexual pleasure – and being a highly adaptable species, we find it in a huge variety of ways. In an era when there is less need than there once was to be "fruitful and multiply," it seems absurd, to say the least, to regard homosexuality as a problem. Unless you regard heterosexuality as a problem, too – in which case perhaps you have a personal problem.

14
Full Circle

"I GROW OLD, I grow old. I shall wear the bottoms of my trousers rolled. Shall I part my hair behind? Do I dare to eat a peach?" J. Arthur Prufrock's timid cry is T. S. Eliot's view of age. Robert Browning's in *Rabbi Ben Ezra* is less pessimistic. "Grow old along with me, the best is yet to be, the last of life for which the first was made."

Byron, however, in *Childe Harold's Pilgrimage*, expressed how it felt not having someone to grow old alongside: "What is the worst of woes that wait on age? What stamps the wrinkle deeper on the brow? To view each loved one blotted from life's page, and be alone on earth, as I am now . . . "Years steal fire from the mind, as vigour from the limb, and life's enchanted cup, but sparkles near the brim."

We fear age for many reasons. The risk of loss which has haunted us from the moment we lose the haven of our mother's uterus looms larger as children depart into adulthood, sexuality departs into fatigue and life itself threatens to leave us and so blot out the universe.

In some societies, where age is respected, even revered, and where old people have a role to fulfill, age brings with it gains to offset these losses, real or threatened. Not being able to have an orgasm matters less to a man who sits enthroned at the head of his family, deferred to and consulted on all important matters, than it does to the man who is at best ignored by his descendants, at worst jeered and cast off.

Our society opts for the latter attitude. The great sin, one sometimes thinks when reading contemporary newspapers and magazines and watching movies and plays, is to be old. At thirty a man is made to feel he ought to be at the top of the hill. By thirty-five he is undoubtedly slithering helplessly down the other side on the way to slipperdom.

For women it is even worse. The thirtieth birthday is regarded with such horror that jokes about being twenty-nine forever are common currency. (Personally, I was so irritated by the people who sniggered when I said I was twenty-nine that I chose to say I was thirty a year before I actually was.)

We also place an excessively high value on sexual potency. The ability to share sexual pleasure and to have an orgasm is an agreeable one, and most of us would be sorry not to have it; but going by our more popular journals and many widely selling books, it is almost a religious duty these days. The hunt for the "Great O" for women and the "Inexhaustible Erection" for men has become a Holy Grail for far too many.

Yet age is ineluctable. The only alternative we have is premature death, and most of us fear that even more than wrinkles. This being so, why on earth do we make it so much harder for ourselves by turning age into something to be shunned and avoided, to be kept at bay by wearing clothes that look great on fifteen-year-olds, ludicrous on fifty-fives; having hair transplants, face lifts, misery-inducing dieting regimes and all the rest of the claptrap born of the youth culture?

The most absurd thing about such behavior is that even if it does manage to persuade others that we are ten years younger than we actually are, we don't convince ourselves. When a man lies awake in bed at night worrying about his sexual potency, or a woman sits and stares into her mirror, counting her wrinkles, where is the satisfaction in having conned a few out-siders during the day? Nowhere. In fact, it makes the truth about your age even more difficult to face.

If people in their middle years were less terrified of growing old, they would probably have fewer problems about relating to their young adult children. But all too often relations are strained because of the attempt by the older generation to remain young – which means they set themselves up in sexual competition with their own sons and daughters.

Dear Claire,

My problem concerns my mother. She used to be a very beautiful woman and could get any man she wanted, which she often did while she was married to my father, who was a very good man. In the end she left my dad for another man, who left his wife and five children for her. They set up home to-gether with me, my brother and sister, but she still flirted with a lot of different men. I knew she was doing this and I hated seeing her doing it, and I often told her about it but she just told me to stop being stupid. When I was growing up she also told me how terrible and dirty sex was and how it hurt her, etc., but she still flirted no end as though she loved it. Even now if she is taking my little boy out, when she passes some workman she always empha-sizes the word granny, so that she'll get a comment on what a young granny she is. I know this is natural, but she wriggles and giggles like a tart. I told her to stop it, she was just showing herself up, but she doesn't listen.

When I first met my husband she hated him and

did everything in her power to stop me from seeing
him. He tried to write to me but she would take the
letters and hide them from me, but then go and
show them to my friend and have a good laugh
about them, yet she could watch me being really
upset wondering why he hadn't written to me. As
you can imagine, my mother and I never got on
very well. I don't know why but we just never did.
There was no specific reason. Anyway, when I was
married we got on very well, me and my husband,
and were very happy. We got a house and had a
little boy and a little girl and we loved each other
very much. He is now twenty-two and I am nineteen, twenty next month. My mother is still the
same as she always was and she is now forty-one.
Her friend who goes to the pub to play darts with
her said that as she's playing darts, the zip on her
dress, which is at the front, comes further and
further down until her bust is showing. Her friend
said one day someone is going to slap her across
the face, the way she acts, but I said it's up to her
how she acts. It's her life – if that's the way she
wants to lead it, it's up to her, and I walked away.
I thought, I've got my own life now and my own
little family. But now she's gone too far. My
husband went over to her place to give her a parcel
from me, and she started her act, which I've seen so
often, the wriggling, the giggling, the rubbing her
hand down her leg, then she sat so that he could
just see her knickers and her bra, and of course she
had her suspenders on. The she sat on his lap and
started kissing his ear. I have told you this in
detail as I want you to understand it was not half
and half, it was *her* fault. I know her, believe me,
and my husband has said he knows now that he
should have just walked out, but he just couldn't

and I believe him. I was willing not to say a thing about this as I thought, she's bound to regret it now and be sorry, but now I've heard she's telling everyone about it, saying he made a pass at her! I'm sorry to say this, but I really hate her and I feel like going to her house and telling her exactly what I think of her, but she would only make a mountain out of that, so I don't know what to do. I love my husband very much, but eventually I'm sure this will break us up, already our sex life is nil. Every time I kiss him I think of him kissing her and it makes me feel sick. He tries to understand but he's losing his patience a bit now. I can't talk to my father about it, because my husband works for him and that would make life impossible for him. I'm trying hard to just pity her, to think that she must be sick in the head to do that to her own daughter, but her telling people doesn't make that easy.

When the drive to maintain sexuality at a young level puts a woman in direct competition with her adult daughter (or for that matter, a man with his adult son) the situation can be painful for the younger person, but not beyond her or his ability to understand and cope. But sometimes, unfortunately, an older man may seek reassurance and sexual gratification within the family in a potentially very destructive way.

Dear Claire,
    Please help me to decide what to do. We have two children, Jeanette and Janice, and they are five and seven. My husband and I are a very happy couple, and had always been very relaxed about sex with the children, answering their questions when they asked them, not being afraid to let them see us nude, etc. So

what happened can't have been something that was our fault, or our daughter's fault, I'm sure of that.

Well, my husband's parents live a few streets away from us, and we've always got on quite well. My mother-in-law has been a bit difficult, ever since she had a hysterectomy a few years ago, and I know she expects my father-in-law to pay a lot of attention to her, and so do we, really. He's been retired for three years – he's now sixty-eight – and used to be with the railroad as a senior official. He's always been a healthy, active sort of man, and is always willing to do anything for anyone. He dug up our garden and planted it for us when we moved to this house, which was brand new, and did a lot of carpentry for us, etc., and we were very grateful.

When he was building some cupboards for the children's bedroom, a job which he knew was going to take three weeks, I was asked to do a little job, as a demonstrator at an exhibition. The money was good and it sounded interesting, and when Granddad offered to look after the girls, as it was school vacation, and my husband said it would be a good idea, I decided to take it.

Anyway, all seemed all right until one night, a week after the little job was over and I was bathing Jeannette. She pulled away from me when I started to wash her bottom. I asked her what was the matter, did she hurt? because she was behaving so oddly. And she burst into tears and said she didn't like it, because Granddad did that and she didn't like it. Well, naturally I asked her what she meant, and after a while she told me, and I truly didn't nag or put words into her mouth or anything.

It turned out he'd been touching her sex organs, and pushing his finger into her and then when she cried he held her on his lap, and – this made me really sick, it really did – he undid his trousers and got her to touch his penis, and Jeannette said he acted very strangely and then gave her ten cents and said not to tell anyone.

I couldn't believe it, I really couldn't, and I didn't know what to do. Well, I told my husband in the end – I felt I had to – and he was all for going around to his father's to beat him up, but I said to him, what good would that do? We decided to take Jeannette to the doctor's and he was marvelous, examined her very gently and didn't frighten her, and she told him the same thing she told me, and I was glad really, because I was beginning to feel it was me who'd made it all up, that I was the filthy one.

Anyway, the doctor said no harm had been done to Jeannette, physically, and he thought she was all right mentally as well, seeing she could talk about it so easily, but he said it would upset her a lot to make a big thing out of it, that to have a fight with the grand-parents would get us nowhere. He said he'd talk to Granddad for us.

Well, he did, and he asked us to come and see him afterward, and told us that it wasn't really as bad as it all sounded. It seems my mother-in-law since her operation won't have anything to do with sex, not a thing. They have separate beds now, though still in the same room. She sleeps badly, so he can't even find self-release – she wakes up at the least movement in their room – and as the doctor said, my father-in-law is a healthy man with plenty of drive in him still, but a bit timid, and never having had any sex relationship with anyone but my mother-in-law is not the sort to go to another woman. In fact, the doctor said, he's fright-ened of women. That was why he turned to Jeannette – he was even a bit scared of our older one at seven. He felt safe with such a little girl – and it seems he hadn't planned it or anything, it just happened. He meant no harm, but what happened had given him a bit of relief and he'd felt very ashamed afterward. He told the doctor it would never happen again. So the doctor says we should all try to go on as though nothing had happened. He's sure there'll be no more problems. But honestly, how can I? Every time I think of the old man, let alone look at him, I feel sick."

Frank expression of sexual need of the sort described in the second of these two letters is alarming and possibly distasteful, but curiously enough this can be easier to handle and understand than the behavior of a parent who seeks to control an adult child's sexuality because it is seen as a painful reminder of the loss of personal attractiveness and sexuality.

There are some women who, around the age of menopause, become very jealous of their children's reproductive ability. The response to this may be either direct, as the first letter shows, or, more commonly, buried to reemerge in a self-serving form.

The classic example of this is the too eager, would-be grandmother. This is the woman who, from the moment her children are old enough, tries to push them into a relationship, and once they marry, nags and questions them constantly about when they are going to have children. Fertility clinics often report that young parents admit parental pressure has brought them in search of help more than their own immediate anxieties. Such women also display an almost prurient interest in the details of the young couple's sex life, disguising this as concern about their ability to conceive. Over the years I have received a very larger number of letters from women asking for help for a daughter's or daughter-in-law's sexual problem. (I refuse to give the advice, incidentally, always saying that I can only do that for people who write themselves, never at second hand.)

Once the younger couple have given in to the pressure and conceived, the mother or mother-in-law then moves in on them (actually into their home, sometimes!) and attempts to take over. She fusses the pregnant girl into believing herself virtually an invalid, offering to deal with her housework, her preparations for the baby and even, where she can, accompanies her on her visits to the doctor for check-ups.

It is difficult for a young woman to resist such actions. Unless she has had a previous pregnancy or is unusually self-reliant and informed, she feels unsure of herself and is grateful for support during what can be an alarming experience. If this older woman, who has herself been through the same experience, warns her that she will feel ill if she does so and so, will damage her baby if she doesn't do this and this, she tends to believe her. She can be made, in fact, to feel ill when she need not; pregnancy is not, after all, an unhealthy activity, but a normal physiological process. And the girl has no reason to see the older woman's actions as prompted by anything but the purest altruism. After all, what is there in it for her but extra work and worry, while the young one lies and rests in peace and comfort?

In fact there is a lot in it for her, as the younger mother will eventually find out. If she is allowed to, this sort of older woman will virtually annex the pregnancy for herself, experiencing it vicariously. If the hospital agrees, she will try to remain with the daughter or daughter-in-law in labor; where the delivery is carried out in the home rather than a hospital, then she indeed reigns supreme.

Afterward, this sort of mother (or mother-in-law) is very likely to try to dissuade the young mother from breast-feeding. She will tell alarming tales of breast abscess and figure loss, and when the baby is the least bit fractious or restless, will ascribe that to the failure of the mother's milk (which is ridiculous, of course).

Not until the baby is established on bottle feeding is she happy, and then she does all she can "to save you trouble, dear. I'll feed him." It can take a considerable effort of will on the part of a young woman, who may already be suffering from a degree of postpartum depression, to resist all this militant unselfishness.

Of course what is happening is far from unselfish. For the once young woman, now middle aged, is able to play at being young again by such ploys, and dearly does she enjoy it, and much does she gain from it. (Remember Naomi and Ruth?)

And woe betide the young family in which there are two such mothers in action.

Whether a woman tries to take over the sexual or reproductive life of a young couple, or a man tries to find sexual release in some sort of incestuous way rather than outside the family, both are acting as they do for the same reason. They are trying to stave off death. According to Professor Edward Wilson of Harvard University, who coined the word "sociobiology," we are all driven by the selfish gene – that the survival of our genes in our own bodies, or in those of our children, matters more to us than anything else, that altruism, morality and justice are not man's triumphant statement of his desire for perfection, but social constructs to enable our precious genes to survive longer.

Certainly when one observes the machinations of some older people – desperately trying to stave off the loss of sexuality, through which, of course, the selfish gene is reproduced, and equally desperately involving themselves in the sexuality and reproductive behavior of their offspring (once again the route through which the genes are passed to yet another generation) the theory, for all its unpleasant political implications, becomes plausible.

It is interesting that much of the desperate fighting against the threat of ageing that appears in the behavior of some middle-aged people (and let me make it clear that I am not trying to castigate an entire age group: for every fifty-year-old who behaves as I have here described, there are of course many others who do not!) disappears when old age is an established fact.

People of fifty seem far more frightened of dying than people of seventy, who have a greater reason to be alarmed. It is people of fifty who give up smoking and eating butter and cheese and enroll in jogging classes. People of seventy do not.

Is it because they have cheated death by reaching the full biblical life span? Hardly! Life is always precious, and always has been. As Seneca said in pre-Christian Rome: "No one's so old that he mayn't with decency hope for one more day," and long before him Sophocles said, "No one loves life like an old man." Philosophers and other thinkers have rediscovered this same truth in every succeeding generation. So, why should old people be more accepting of their aged state than those who are just about to enter it?

Surely it is that once age is established, and the loss of sexuality – the ability to pass on that selfish gene – has happened, the individual is no longer driven so hard. The gene-passing days have gone and that's that. Whether there are grandchildren or not they have done all they can to give their special genes a future. He or she has come to terms with life as it is now rather than the way it used to be. The old person discovers that there are other pleasures to be found in life without sex; there is food and drink, for a start. The greed of old people is well recognized. There is also sleep, and time,

time that can be used for self-indulgence, rather than for the pursuit of self-gratification.

And it adds up to a lot of time, when you come to think of it. The amount of effort that young men and women put into achieving an orgasm, if you measure it from the very start when two possible sexual partners meet, is colossal. And for what? A few seconds of physical sensation. Intense, and agreeable of course – but so short! So little of it! Old people, the wise and happy ones, know this, and live their time to better advantage than they ever did when they were young.

Browning was right, surely: "Grow old along with me, the best is yet to be. The best of life, for which the first was made."

Bibliography

BOOKS

Kinship and Marriage, Fox, R., Penguin, Harmondsworth, 1968.

Totem and Taboo, Freud, S. (translated by James Strachey), Routledge and Kegan Paul, Henley-on-Thames, 1950. First published 1913.

Comparative Studies in Kinship, Goody, J., Routledge and Kegan Paul, 1969.

Sex and Repression in Savage Society, Malinowski, B., Routledge and Kegan Paul, 1927.

History of Human Marriage, Westermarck, E., Macmillan, London, 1889.

Incest, Maisch, H. (translated by Colin Bearne), Andre Deutsch, London, 1973.

Sexual Behavior in the Human Male, Kinsey, A. C.; Pomeroy, W. B.; Martin, C., Saunders, Philadelphia, 1948.

Incest Behavior, Weinberg, S. K., Citadel Press, New York, 1955.

Life, Zeno, Pan Books, London.

Incest, Mead, M., International Encyclopaedia of the Social Sciences, Cromwell, Collier and Macmillan, New York, 1968.

Sexual Offences (NCCL Report No. 13): Evidence to the Criminal Law Revision Committee, National Council for Civil Liberties, London, 1976.

PAPERS

Incest, Noble, M., Mason, J. K., *Journal of Medical Ethics,* 1978, Vol. 4, No. 2, P. 64.

The Varieties of Incest, Bagley, C., *New Society,* August 21, 1968, P. 28.

Sibling Incest, Fox, J. R., *British Journal of Sociology,* 1962, Vol. 13, P. 128.

The Incest Taboo in Relation to Social Structure and the Socialisation of the Child, Parsons, T., *British Journal of Sociology,* 1962, Vol. 13, P. 125.

Incest: New Findings, Browning, D. H., Boatman, B., *American Journal of Psychiatry,* 1977, Vol. 134, P. 69-72.

Sexual Abuse Begins at Home, Weber, E., *Ms* Magazine, April 1977, P. 64.

Incest, Inbreeding and Mental Abilities, Roberts, D. F., *British Medical Journal,* 1967, Vol. 4, P. 336-337.

Incest and Family Disorder (Editorial, no author quoted), *British Medical Journal,* May 13, 1972, P. 364-365.

Index

abortion, 37, 74
Abraham, 13
adolescence, 176–9, 184–5, 190–200
advertising, fantasy images, 25
aging, 239–60
Albee, Edward, *Who's Afraid of Virginia Woolf?*, 84
'Alex', 90–2, 135–40
'Alice', 83–4
Allen, Woody, 192
American Humane Association, 205
'Andrew', 64–6, 177
'Anna', 151–5
anorexia nervosa, 160–2
Austen, Jane, *Pride and Prejudice*, 125

babies, maternal relationships, 89–98
bar mitzvah, 12
'Barbara', 16–21, 176–7
'Bill J.', 213–14
Boaz, 57–8
Booker, Bob, 14

breasts, changes due to pregnancy, 85, 87
'Bridie', 100–4
British Medical Association (BMA), 216
brother/sister relationships, 145–64, 167–70
brothers-in-law, 67–70
'Brown, Dr', 27–35
Browning, Robert, *Rabbi Ben Ezra*, 239, 250
Bugsy Malone, 206
Byron, Lord, *Childe Harold's Pilgrimage*, 239

Catholic church, 14, 71
'Cathy', 77–80
'Cecily', 171–5
'Charles', 163–4
child pornography, 205–6
child-stealing, 81
childlessness, 71, 80–4, 87–8
children, and marriage, 71–88

Chinatown, 206
'Christine', 196
cinema, fantasy images, 25
clothing, children's, 134; transvestites, 220–31
coitus interruptus, 37
contraception, 36–7; in adolescence, 186–7; loss of libido, 36
'Cooper, Mrs', 142, 143
corporal punishment, 183–4
couvade, 106
'Cyril', 151–5

'Danny', 64–6, 95–6
'Daphne', 171–5
daughter/father relationships, 133–44, 188, 190–1, 197–9, 206–7, 202–17
daughter/mother relationships, 92–7, 122–32, 185–7, 199–200
'David', 42–8

Davis, Bette, 75, 234–5
'Debbie', 95–7
Deceased Wife's Sister Marriage Act (1907), 69–70
'Diane', 163–4
Dickens, Charles, 69
Dickens, Kate, 69
'dieting disease', 160–2
discipline, children, 182–4
'Donald', 77–9, 135–9
'Donna', 135–9
'Dorothy', 58–64
drag shows, 220
Dunaway, Faye, 206

'Edith', 164–7
'Edward', 116–121
Egypt, ancient, 168
Eliot, T. S., 239
extended family, 12–15, 24–5

family, structure of, 10–25
Family Life, 237
father/daughter relationships, 133–44, 188, 190–1, 197–9, 202–17
father/son relationships, 105–21, 188, 197, 200
fathers-in-law, 57
fertility clinics, 80–1
flagellation, 183–4
Foster, George, 14
Foster, Jodi, 205
Freud, Sigmund, 10, 11, 203, 218, 237
frigidity, 202

Funny Girl, 42

Gabor sisters, 70
'Gary', 100–4
Gay Liberation, 235–6
gender differences, 89–94, 131–2, 150
'Gerald', 163–4
Gibben, Trevor, 215
girls, as sex objects, 133–5
'Gloria', 58–64
gonorrhea, 83
'Gordon J.', 211–12
Greece, ancient, 11, 39, 236–7
Grenfell, Joyce, 150
Guinness Book of Records, 85

'Harold', 192–3
'Helen', 135–40
hemophilia, 168
'Henry', 59–63
hereditary diseases, 167–8
Hilton, James, *Goodbye Mr. Chips*, 84
Hogarth, Georgina, 69
homosexuality, 52, 111, 170–1, 235–8
Huston, John, 206
hysterectomy, loss of libido, 36

'Ian', 192–6
inbreeding, 167–9, 216
incest, 69–70, 157–62, 167–75, 202–19
incontinence, due to pregnancy, 86
inheritance, 109
in-laws, 56–70

Ireland, brothers-in-law, 67–8; extended families, 14
'Irving', 151–5
Italy, brothers-in-law, 68; extended family, 13, 15

'Jack', 166–7
'James', 176
'Jan', 111–20
The Jazz Singer, 106
jealousy, sibling, 146–8, 170
'Jenkins, Dr', 30–1, 33
'Jessica', 151–5
Jews, extended families, 14; parents-in-law, 56
'Joel', 95–8
'John', 232–4
'John K.', 210–11, 214–15
Jolson, Al, 106
Jung, C. G., 203

'Keith', 53
'Kerry', 176
King, Hetty, 231
Kinsey, 182
Kiss Me Kate, 189

Laing, R. D., 237
The Lancet, 223–6
'Lawrence', 26–36
Lawrence, D. H., *Sons and Lovers*, 218
laws of consanguinity, 69
'Lena', 155–8
lesbians, 236–7
libido, loss of, 36;

in pregnancy,
  76–7
Lilith, 39
Loach, Ken, 237
London, 68

MacNaughton, Bill,
  The Anniversary,
  234–5
maiden aunts, 68
Margaret, Princess,
  217
'Marie', 95–8
marriage,
  childbearing,
  71–88; childless,
  71, 80–4, 87–8;
  sex in, 42–55
'Mary', 140–4, 172–5
Masters and
  Johnson sex
  therapy, 20, 196
masturbation, 182
matriarchy, 13–14,
  22–4
Me Mammy, 99–100
Mediterranean, 13
menopause, 246;
  loss of libido, 36
menstruation, 72, 73
'Michael', 50–1,
  100–4
'Michelle', 42–8
'Mile High Club', 44
miscarriages, 74
Mr. Skeffington, 75
money and sex,
  37–41
mother/daughter
  relationships, 92–8,
  122–32, 185–7,
  199–200
mother/son
  relationships,
  89–104, 187, 188,
  191–6, 217–19

mothers-in-law,
  56–66
MS, 205
myths, 11, 39

names, significance
  of, 108–9
'Naomi', 26–36
Naomi (Biblical),
  57–8
National
  Association of the
  Childfree, 81
National
  Organization of
  Non Parents
  (NON), 81
Nesbit, E., *Five
  Children and It*,
  150; *The Phoenix
  and the Carpet*,
  150
*New York, New
  York*, 74, 77
Nicholls, Peter,
  *Privates on
  Parade*, 238
'Nina', 64–6
No, No, Nanette, 122
*No Way To Treat a
  Lady*, 235
Noah, 13
nuclear family,
  14–15, 24–5

Oedipus myth, 218
old age, 239–50
orgasm, 240; male,
  38
osteogenesis
  imperfecta, 168

parenthood, 71–88
parents-in-law,
  56–67
patriarchy, 12–13,

108–9
'Patty', 90–2
'Paul', 113–20
'Peter', 16–21
'Peter S.', 212–13
Pinter, Harold, *The
  Lover*, 48–9
Play It Again, Sam,
  192
pornography, 50–1;
  child, 205–6
Porter, Cole, 189
pregnancy, 71–88,
  105–6; and
  woman's
  sexuality, 36–7
premarital sex, 71–2
Pretty Baby, 205–6
prostitution, 39
puberty, 120, 176–9,
  184, 191–200;
  rituals of, 12
Pulse, 215–17
Punch, 68
punishment,
  children, 182–4
Pusey, Edward
  Bouverie, 69–70

Rains, Claude, 75
'Ray', 111–20
rite de passage, 21
Rome, ancient, 11,
  39, 236
Roth, Philip,
  *Portnoy's
  Complaint*, 192,
  218
Ruth, 57–8

'Sam', 83–4
'Sandra', 21–4
Sappho, 237
'Sarah', 158–62
schizophrenia,
  237–8

Segal, George, 235
Seneca, 249
sex education,
185–6, 188–9
sexual equality,
90–3, 150
Shakespeare,
William, *Hamlet*,
11, 41, 218;
Romeo and Juliet,
66
sheaths,
contraceptive, 37
'Sheila', 192–6
sibling
relationships,
145–75
'Simon', 158–62
single-parent
families, 140–4
sister/brother
relationships,
145–64, 167–70
sister/sister
relationships,
164–7, 170–5
sisters-in-law, 67–70
'Smith family',
151–5
Sodom, 236
song lyrics, 188–90
son/father

relationships,
105–21, 188, 197,
200
son/mother
relationships,
89–104, 187,
188–9, 191–6,
217–19
Sophocles, 249
Steiger, Rod, 235
step-children, 82–3
sterilization, loss of
libido, 36
stillbirth, 74, 81
Strachey, Lytton,
169–70
Streisand, Barbra,
42
'Susan', 64–6, 140–4
Swinburne,
Algernon, 183

'Tables of Affinity',
69
Taxi Driver, 205
Taylor, Brooke,
205–6
'Ted', 21–4
television, fantasy
images, 25
'Thomas', 155–8
Tilley, Vesta, 231

toddlers, maternal
relationships,
98–9
toilet training,
179–82
Toulouse-Lautrec,
Henri, 168
transsexuals, 231–4
transvestites, 53,
220–31, 234–5
Trollope, Anthony,
Dr. Thorne, 38–9

vagina, changes
due to pregnancy,
86, 87
vaginismus, 16–17,
202
venereal disease, 83
Victoria, Queen of
England, 168
'Violet', 164–7

Wilson, Edward,
248
Wordsworth,
William, *Ode on
Intimations of
Immortality*, 179

*You Don't Have to
be Jewish*, 14, 39, 67